# CATALOG OF HUMAN SOULS
## Book 5

## SHAN HAI JING—A BOOK COVERED WITH BLOOD

### The Story Of Developers Of The Catalog Of Human Population

Kate Bazilevsky

**HPA Press**

ISBN-10: 0996731245

ISBN-13: 978-0-9967312-4-9

Kate Bazilevsky

**Shan Hai Jing—A Book Covered With Blood: The Story Of Developers Of The Catalog Of Human Population.**

Chapters 2-4 translated by Anonymous.

Chapters 5 and 6 translated by Kate Bazilevsky.

*Dedicated to the 40ᵗʰ anniversary of the discovery of the
Catalog of Human Population by researcher Andrey Davydov.*

# Table of Contents

# PREFACE

We—authors of the Catalog of Human Souls book series—would like to briefly describe what these books are about right from the beginning because the topic of the Catalog of Human Population is very new for many people.

These books are dedicated to the 40<sup>th</sup> anniversary from the beginning of research that led to discovery of the Catalog of Human Population. A technology of uncovering of the individual structure of human psyche (or simply put—the soul) was created on the basis of this scientific discovery. The author of scientific discovery of the Catalog of Human Population and this technology is a researcher of ancient books, an expert in Chinese culture Andrey Davydov.

The source of knowledge about the structure of human psyche and the basis for creation of this technology is one of the most ancient and mysterious texts preserved in this civilization—the ancient Chinese monument Shan Hai Jing (translated as the Catalog of Mountains and Seas), which Andrey Davydov managed to decrypt.

After Andrey Davydov created the technology of decryption of Shan Hai Jing (Catalog of Mountains and Seas), it was found that this ancient Chinese monument contains very detailed descriptions of 293 models of human psyche and a lot of other kind of information about the structure of *Homo sapiens*. On this basis, Shan Hai Jing was qualified as the Catalog of Human Population.

In Shan Hai Jing (Catalog Mountains and Seas), the biological type "human" is described as a type divided into 293 subtype structures according to the phenological principle. It turned out that each person, belonging to one of these 293 subtypes from birth, has stable characteristics of this subtype; regardless of race, nationality and particularities of parental psychophysiological structures, which are only minor correctors.

Information about the subtype structure is implanted in the form of a program in the unconscious of a person from birth, and this program determines all of his life: his/her personal qualities and character properties, algorithms of life and functioning, hidden motivational spring, abilities, talents, preferences, inclinations, etc. Natural subtype program is that what is called "psyche", "soul."

Natural program is that individuality, which makes a person different from other people as representatives of other subtype structures of biological type *Homo sapiens*. Each individual "speaks his own language," specified by his subtype program, as the language of values, views, convictions, preferences, which are standard and unchanging for all representatives of a subtype.

In the language of science, a natural subtype program of *Homo sapiens* is called Individual Archetypal Pattern; in simple language—an Individual (Subtype) Program, an Individual Program or a Program.

A human program is recorded in the language of natural images. Images or, using the language of science, archetypes of the unconscious sphere of a person is the language of human "software." The concept of "an archetype" was introduced to psychology by Carl Gustav Jung, but as it turned out, archetypes can be not only of the collective unconscious, but also individual. Therefore, to avoid confusion, in popular texts we prefer to call the language of "software" of *Homo sapiens* by the word "image" instead of "archetype."

Programs of each of 293 human subtypes are recorded by different natural images and a different number of images, meaning that they are endemic, are not similar to one another. *Homo sapiens* is a living system, which, as it turned out, exists and functions strictly on the basis of a natural program implanted from birth, and from this it was concluded that a human is a bio-robot at the genetic level.

The conclusion that "*Homo sapiens* is a bio-robot" is confirmed by that learning someone's natural individual (subtype) program from the Catalog of Mountains and Seas as the Catalog of Human Population, it is possible to find out absolutely everything about this person in great detail; about any aspect of his life and activities, including that what he or she carefully conceals.

In addition, *Homo sapiens*, as a biosystem programmed by nature, has modes of self-regulation and regulation (control from the outside). Modes of regulation are a natural inborn mechanism, just like an individual human program. Their discoverer Andrey Davydov named these modes Individual Manipulation Modes (Manipulation Modes for short). This management tool, which can be applied to any person, also was found in the text of the ancient Chinese monument Shan Hai Jing.

It was found that for every person, as a biosystem, there are three manipulation modes: suppressing, balancing and stimulating. Manipulation modes together with an individual (subtype) program are individual structure of psyche of *Homo sapiens*. Programs and manipulation modes of each subtype differ, from one another. For this reason, people differ from each other by internal characteristics, and individual manipulation scenarios are necessary for each person.

Structure Of Psyche Of *Homo Sapiens*

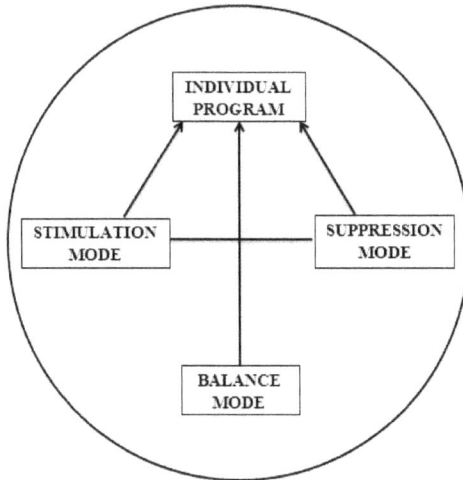

© 2015 Olga Skorbatyuk, Kate Bazilevsky

Individual program, with which a person was born, is the main segment of structure of human psyche (soul). Knowing the natural individual program allows you to find out who he/she (or you personally) is real, without masks, what motives drive this person (or you), and so on.

Suppression mode is a self-control mode, which turns on automatically as a mode of relaxation, pleasure, dream, happy oblivion (a "turn off" button). It is the individual program of people, who belong to a particular subtype. When a manipulator acts out a personality from the suppression mode, it makes an individual experience pleasure, unconsciously get attached to the manipulator (fall in love, etc.), and on this basis obey him/her and fulfill all of his/her requests/demands.

Balance mode is a self-control mode, which turns on automatically when a person needs to become balanced, get in a harmonious, comfortable state without loss of activeness. It is the individual program of people, who belong to a particular subtype. When a manipulator acts out a personality from the balance mode, it makes an individual experience comfort in communication with him/her, trust him/her at the unconscious level and consider him/her the best friend.

Stimulation mode is a self-control mode, which turns on automatically when a person needs to stimulate himself/herself to some actions, become active. It is the individual program of people, who belong to a particular subtype. When a manipulator transmits properties of the stimulation mode in a certain way, it makes an individual experience strong irritation, up to wild rage, and on this basis he/she does that what a manipulator asks for/demands.

Natural manipulation modes described in Shan Hai Jing (Catalog of Mountains and Seas) as the Catalog of Human Population provide a key to managing any person. With the help of knowledge of human manipulation modes, it is possible to factually change a person's physical and psychological state, behavior, reactions in the desired direction.

No one is able to resist application of his personal manipulation modes because it is a natural mechanism, which is built into human psyche from birth. Therefore, information about manipulation modes of a subtype provides unlimited possibilities for influencing any individual as a representative of this subtype and allows self-control and control of any human as a biosystem.

Non-traditional psychoanalysis, a new direction in scientific psychology, allows identifying an individual's subtype structure (psyche) and manipulation modes on the basis of the Catalog of Human Population. It is called non-traditional because it does not use any of the traditional principles, approaches to the study of human psyche, as well as methods (observation, experiment, testing, biographical method, questioning, conversation) since these methods are not needed in order to obtain any kind of information about a person as a stable and identifiable biosystem.

A non-traditional psychoanalyst knows what a person is like, what problems might concern him or her and why, and how these problems can be effectively solved without any kind of contact with this person. All that a non-traditional psychoanalyst needs to know about the subject being studied is the day, the month, the year of his or her birth and the gender. Neither race nor nationality or place of residence of the person being studied matter because the Catalog of Human Population contains descriptions of unchanging characteristics of subtypes of *Homo sapiens* of the entire human population.

For colleagues from the scientific environment we are offering our definition of what human psyche and the Catalog of Human Population are: "*The Catalog of Human Population is a description of a human as a type by subtype structures. Subtype structure ("psyche", "soul") is a combination of individual archetypes, recorded at the genetic level (principle). Expressions and interaction of subtype structures in manipulation modes and phenological algorithms are described with adjustments for gender, age and cultural differences. Information is recorded on six factors.*" This definition was developed by Andrey Davydov—the author of discovery and decryption of the Catalog of Human Population.

It is also necessary to tell a bit about the main source of knowledge (knowledge of that *Homo sapiens* are bio-robots, that human psyche (soul) is "software," that "software" of any person can be easily uncovered, and so on), which was obtained in the course of our scientific research. To date, no one knows for sure who gave and preserved this knowledge, but after it was written down it got the title 山海經 Shan Hai Jing (translated from Chinese as Canon/Catalog of Mountains and Seas).

According to Artem I. Kobzev (a Russian historian of Chinese philosophy, Doctor of Philosophical Sciences, professor, author of over eight hundred scientific papers on the history of Chinese philosophy, science and culture), Shan Hai Jing is an anonymous monument, which presumably dates back to the late III century BC-early II century BC. It consists of eighteen juan (scrolls), combined into two sections: Canon/Book of the Mountains (Shan Jing) or Canon of Five Innermost Mountains (Wu Zang Jing) in five juan and Canon of the Seas (Hai Jing) in thirteen juan.

Legend claims that Shan Hai Jing was engraved on sacred vessels by Bo Yi—an assistant to the wise semi-mythical ruler of the ancient times Yu the Great, who lived in the XXIII century BC. Yu the Great entered the throne in 2205 BC. Authors of the Han epoch attribute authorship of the literary monument Shan Hai Jing to Yu the Great and his companion Bo Yi.

According to legend, Yu the Great dealt with a great flood, which fell upon earth and arranged it. The deedful ruler allegedly came to know its mountains, rivers, their spirits, as well as animals and plants. He ordered his assistant to describe everything that was seen. As a result, these recordings together with images of spirits, fantastic animals, birds and plants were engraved on nine ritual vessels-tripods. Later on, these sacred vessels were lost. However, according to historical annals, prior to their strange disappearance, the text of the Catalog of Mountains and Seas, along with amazing images of representatives of flora and fauna, spirits and deities were copied.

This answers the question why some date Shan Hai Jing back to III-II centuries BC, while others back to XXIII century BC—the Catalog of Mountains and Seas as the source of information appeared during the time of Yu the Great and it got the form of a text much later. We tend to agree with those researchers, who date Shan Hai Jing back to XXIII BC since according to Dan Zhu the Catalog of Mountains and Sea was recorded only after its long-term oral existence (this point of view is expressed in his commentaries to the famous monument Spring and Autumn - Chunqiu). Reports that Yu the Great and his assistant Bo Yi created the Catalog of Mountains and Seas exist in, for example, Wang Chong's (27-97 AD) treatise titled Critical Essays: "When Yu and Bo Yi were taming the waters of the flood—Yu was engaged in calming the water, while Bo Yi in recording information about various "things." And, they created the Catalog of Mountains and Seas."

We will add that apparently in mythologies of almost all cultures of the world (those, which to continue to exist, as well as those, which already sank into oblivion) exist facts, which show that the Catalog of Human Population was present in these cultures. This is not difficult to trace by carefully studying the ancient, archaic cultural layers. However, the source itself was preserved only in one culture—the culture of China. This is not surprising since Chinese culture is not only ancient, but also, in spite of everything, the Chinese manage to preserve it and their traditions from the ancient times to the present day (unlike representatives of other cultures).

This was a brief description of the main points, about which you will be able to learn in detail from the Catalog of Human Souls book series.

*****

In essence, the Catalog of Human Souls book series is one book divided into five parts. All these parts are devoted to a single topic—scientific discovery made by researcher Andrey Davydov, the Catalog of Human Population. Division into five parts was done because materials for this book are quite non-uniform in content and style.

The book Catalog of Human Souls is divided into five parts since fundamental research being carried out by Andrey Davydov and our colleagues is interdisciplinary, and the field of research is wide and multifaceted (psychology, gender relations, sociology, political science, linguistics, sinology and so on), and also because we present results of this research not only in the language of science, but also in the language of popular science.

In addition, we (authors of Catalog of Human Souls books), who are presenting research and discoveries of our laboratory's research supervisor Andrey Davydov, found it necessary to include some information about him as well. It seemed to us that the story of discovery of the Catalog of Human Population might be of interest not only to those, who are already familiar with it, but also to those, who are just learning about the Catalog.

Also, in order not to sound groundless, we decided to offer readers to get acquainted with some of materials from the Catalog of Human Population. These materials are provided in the form of brief demonstration versions from descriptions of natural programs of people. We are of the opinion that presentation of any, even the most captivating scientific theory is, as the saying goes, not worth even a straw, if this theory cannot be tested and used on practice.

Demos that we presented certainly are very short and they are by no means complete descriptions of individuals. However, perhaps they will be quite enough for independent testing, which even a non-professional in the field of psychology will be able to do and get a confirmation that the Catalog of Human Souls (a nonscientific title of the Catalog of Human Population) really exists. And, this means that now he or she can use this Catalog in daily life.

We—authors of the Catalog of Human Souls book series—have the honor to not only tell about some of the research done by our laboratory's research supervisor Andrey Davydov and our colleagues, but also to participate in the development of the Catalog of Human Population. However, it must be stated right away that in all sections where we tell about the technology, methodology of non-traditional psychoanalysis—we are only narrators. Technology of decryption of the ancient Chinese monument Shan Hai Jing was created over 20 years ago and its authorship belongs to Andrey Davydov.

*****

The Catalog of Human Souls book series contains the following five books:

**Book 1. *Homo Sapiens* Are Bio-Robots. Human "Software"** (by Olga Skorbatyuk and Kate Bazilevsky). This book tells about the new method of obtaining information from the unconscious sphere of a human and about the Catalog of Human Population in the form of answers to the most frequently asked questions. In this book, we also presented three hundred selected research topics, which were developed in our laboratory between 1974 and 2014.

**Book 2. Hack Anyone's Soul. 100 Demos Of Human Programs From The Catalog Of Human Population** (by Olga Skorbatyuk and Kate Bazilevsky). In this book, we are offering one hundred brief demonstration versions taken from descriptions of human programs in the Catalog of Human Population. Of course, these descriptions are only a tiny fraction of information that the Catalog contains about each person. However, we think that this is enough for independent testing and to obtain confirmation of existence of the Catalog of Human Population.

**Book 3. Human Manipulation Modes. Either You Are Manipulating Or You Are Being Manipulated** (by Olga Skorbatyuk and Kate Bazilevsky). This book is entirely devoted to manipulation modes—the natural toolkit for controlling a system called "a human," which was discovered in the ancient Chinese monument Shan Hai Jing (which turned out to be the Catalog of Human Population). In this book, we explain what individual manipulation modes are and how to use them to manipulate people. After all, with the discovery of the Catalog of Human Population, only two positions in society are left—either you are manipulating or you are being manipulated. And, as proof of that this is really so, in this book we provided the scenario of suppression mode for manipulation of people, who were born on October 12th of leap years or October 13th of common years. Despite that this is only one of four modes of manipulation of those people, who were born on the dates indicated—it will be sufficient for testing.

**Book 4. Non-Traditional Psychoanalysis. Selected Scientific Articles And Presentations at Conferences** (by Andrey Davydov and Olga Skorbatyuk). This book presents some of the scientific articles and presentations at scientific conferences done by Andrey Davydov, the author of scientific discovery of the Catalog of Human Population. It also includes several scientific articles (which are also chapters of the textbook titled Archetypal Pattern. Fundamentals of Non-Traditional Psychoanalysis.), authors of which are founders of non-traditional psychoanalysis: Andrey Davydov and his colleague—psychologist Olga Skorbatyuk.

**Book 5. Shan Hai Jing—A Book Covered With Blood. The Story Of Developers of the Catalog of Human Population** (by Kate Bazilevsky). This book uncovers the story of developers of the Catalog of Human Population—Andrey Davydov and Olga Skorbatyuk— that is related to obtaining of political asylum in the United States of America due to many years of persecution by the Federal Security Service of Russian Federation (FSB, former KGB) and attempts to kill them in order to take possession of their research product—the Catalog of Human Population.

*****

From the beginning, as authors of the book series Catalog of Human Souls, we would like to apologize for the lack of a single language style and popular language. Our colleagues from the scientific environment, professional psychologists or those, who are interested in scientific psychology, can satisfy their curiosity about the theory that lies at the basis of technology that we use to identify the individual structure of psyche in Book 4 of this series (Non-Traditional Psychoanalysis. Selected Scientific Articles And Presentations At Conferences.).

The other four books in this series are intended for the widest audience. From our point of view, any person, regardless of education level, must have an opportunity to get acquainted with results of our research. After all, Shan Hai Jing, as the Catalog of Human Population, was left to all humanity. Therefore, in many of our books (despite that they are all devoted exclusively to scientific topics) we try to use the literary language, avoiding frequent use of specific terminology. However, we were unable not to use jargon at all, and for this we beg your pardon. We are not writers, our main work is scientific research, and in books we are sharing with the audience some of the results of this activity, according to the common practice in the scientific community.

Speaking of language that we use to describe the topic of our research... It was noticed that some people are perplexed by that we use the word "soul," as it is not customary to use this word in the scientific community. However, as it was found, human soul, which is the same as psyche and subtype structure—exists. And, it exists regardless of someone's opinions about it.

Soul (psyche), as "software" of *Homo sapiens* is not a psychological, religious or metaphysical value—as it turned out, it is purely a natural value. Therefore, like any natural phenomenon (rain, wind, electricity, gravity), the soul functions regardless of whether people know about it or not, and regardless of what they think about this. People can argue as much as they want whether soul exists or not, and fantasize as much as they want about what it is, but the natural mechanism called "soul" will continue to work. In every person, while he is alive.

Therefore, every person has the right to continue debating whether or not the soul exists and fantasize about what it is, but we prefer to study the human soul as an existing phenomenon (which, by the way, is possible to see, hear, smell and touch, if you have information about individual structures of psyche) and use results of this research on practice.

We consider the question of what words to use to call the natural phenomenon "soul" unimportant when it is possible to study it as a phenomenon instead of talking about it. We use the word "soul" because in any language it accurately reflects the essence of the phenomenon—that foundation, on the basis of which any human being lives, and because of which he is alive; that what is called "closer than the body." And, unlike our colleagues-psychologists, we are not forgetting that "psychology" translated from the ancient Greek means "science about the soul" (from the ancient Greek ψυχή - "soul," λόγος - "teaching").

\*\*\*\*\*

Now, let's get back to the Catalog of Human Souls books series. Those people, who are already familiar with our research and our other books, usually have questions, to some of which we would like to provide answers in the Catalog of Human Souls book series. For example, people are interested to know who exactly is working on compiling of the Catalog of Human Population, and why it is not possible to find information anywhere, including on the Internet, about all members of our laboratory's staff. Also, people want to know how they can get information from the Catalog of Human Population about themselves or other people.

With regard to the question about developers of the Catalog of Human Population and other staff members of our laboratory, it really is difficult to find reliable information about them and here is why. This happens for two reasons: the first reason is explained using an example with the Internet in the Introduction to Book 1 of this series titled Homo sapiens Are Bio-Robots, and the second reason is confidentiality of all of this kind of information and is related to security. The number people in our laboratory, who work on compiling of the Catalog of Human Population, is not three people, as it might seem. However, unfortunately, we cannot provide any information about who these people are. Reasons for this are detailed in Book 5 of this series (Shan Hai Jing—A Book Covered With Blood. The Story Of Developers Of The Catalog Of Human Population).

Due to persecution because of the main subject of our scientific research— the Catalog of Human Population—by a group of employees of Federal Security Service of Russian Federation (FSB, former KGB), headed by colonel of Foreign Intelligence Service (data for the period 2000-2004) Andrey Dmitrievich Polonchuk, we do not have the right to provide any kind of information about our laboratory's staff. You can get acquainted with the evidence of these prosecutions in Book 5 mentioned above. Originals of documents presented there are stored in the United States Department of Homeland Security, Federal Bureau of Investigation (FBI), etc.

Therefore, if anywhere in public sources, for example on the Internet, you come across a statement that someone is an employee of the Special Scientific Info-Analytical Laboratory—Catalog Of Human Souls or the Human Population Academy, and is engaged in developments related to decryption of Shan Hai Jing and compilation of the Catalog of Human Population—it can be either disinformation or fraud, or both. However, we do have partners and affiliates. Therefore, it is always best to check with us.

Beware that some research works of Andrey Davydov (the author of discovery of the Catalog of Human Population) and the Special Scientific Info-Analytical Laboratory—Catalog Of Human Souls led by him were stolen by a group of employees of the Federal Security Service of Russia (formerly KGB) headed by Andrey Dmitrievich Polonchuk—colonel of SVR FSB of Russian Federation (information about his rank refers to 2000-2004). Therefore, it is possible to find offers on the Internet (in different languages) to purchase information from the Catalog of Human Population, even though this information is in no way related to the Catalog or to natural human "software."

Such offers can be found at the following websites: in Russian – Mountains and Seas of Self-Knowledge http://mountaseas.com, Catalog of Human Population (Catalog of Mountains and Seas) http://vk.com/chp_lab, Find The Answer Within Yourself http://www.facebook.com/groups/mountaseas.2905/, Catalog of Human Population http://vk.com/googlite; in English – Shan Hai Jing Lab/Shan Hai Jing Laboratory http://www.facebook.com/SHJLab/info, http://twitter.com/SHJLab and http://shjlab.wordpress.com; etc.

It is extremely dangerous to buy products offered by fraudsters. Since some time back Andrey Davydov suspected that sooner or later, in one form or another piracy will occur and made some inaccuracies in materials related to Shan Hai Jing; without taking them into account it is impossible to correctly put together the base material.

Perhaps, after realizing this A. D. Polonchuk's group decided to get at least some, at least material benefits from stolen works and this is how a strange, ugly product was born, which has nothing to do with information from the Catalog of Human Population as the decrypted ancient Chinese monument Shan Hai Jing.

The consequence of this is that those, who get information from fraudsters cause irreparable damage to their health; both physical and psychical. Unfortunately, our laboratory already has a significant amount of information about cases when people, who requested information from the Catalog of Human Population from those, who officially have nothing to do with this research, experienced serious damage in various matters and of varying degree of severity. The reason for this is the fact that human psychophysiology functions on the basis of images. Therefore, if a person receives images and decryptions (which essentially are images as well), which are in no way related to his/her personal psychophysiology and begins to use this information on practice, then consequences might be as follows:

- psychical disorders of any kind, which cannot be cured

- somatic disorders of any kind, which cannot be cured

- death, as a result of psychical and physiological disorders

Therefore, please be careful. You have every right to turn to anyone for information from the Catalog, but we issued this warning and we will not be held responsible in any way for possible consequences of your decisions.

You can get information from the Catalog of Human Population about yourself or any other person directly from our laboratory right now. For convenience of our clients, the system of issuance of any kind of information directly from developers of the Catalog of Human Population is made in such a way that they do not need to contact us. Anyone can view prices and pay for an order here - https://www.humanpopulationacademy.org/pricing/.

And, for those people, who would like to not just get materials from the Catalog of Human Population sold on our website, but also contact us (for example, with a business proposal, to order of some specific services, to get consultations, to become a student, etc.)—please refer to Human Population Academy's Contacts page at https://www.humanpopulationacademy.org/breakthrough-discovery/contacts/.

Purchasing information from the Catalog through our website or by contacting us are the only ways to get information from the Catalog of Human Population directly from its developer without the risk of coming across fraudsters.

It should be noted that no one ever persecuted our clients; they never were and are not in any danger because those who persecuted and continue to persecute us were never interested in our clients as they do not have information about the technology of decryption of Shan Hai Jing. In addition, we always respect confidentiality of any person, who turns to us for information from the Catalog and we never share information about our clients with anyone.

*****

In conclusion, we would like to state the principled position that we adhere to as authors of books (and, currently there are over three hundred of them)—we do not in any way claim to be gurus; we are more comfortable with the position of students. However, due to the fact that we engaged and continue to engage in research work, we are able to obtain information that can be interesting and useful not only to us. And, we are just legalizing this information for those, who prefer not to believe, but to know. To know how the world works and what is his or her own, personal structure.

Another principal point is that in our books, we do not share our personal opinions, hypotheses. Everything that we state is information from the ancient sources that we are studying and facts obtained during the course of our research activities, which have been tested, as it is customary in scientific practice. We prefer to keep to ourselves our opinions and fantasies, as insignificant in comparison with that what is stated in our books.

Also, on behalf of our colleagues from the laboratory and ourselves, in celebration of the 40th anniversary since the beginning of research of the ancient Chinese monument Shan Hai Jing as the Catalog of Human

Population, we would like to express deep gratitude to all of our relatives, friends, acquaintances and colleagues from the scientific environment, as well as to all others, whom we happened to come across in life, for that they failed to prevent us from carrying out this research.

*Olga Skorbatyuk and Kate Bazilevsky*
*Los Angeles, California*
*June 2015*

# INTRODUCTION

Although it might seem like someone's figment of imagination, from beginning to end this story is not fiction. This is a documentary story that happened to real people and it tells about the real events of their lives. However, dear fans of fiction, do not rush to close this book, as it describes really fantastic things and events. Fantastic since, first of all, in 99% out of 100% people caught in such circumstances cannot tell anything to anyone anymore because they are no longer alive. Secondly, if we believe historians and archaeologists, then that what happened to people in this story has never before happened to any person, who has ever lived or lives in this civilization.

In essence, this story is about how a certain person was searching his bookshelf for something to read and in the end found a book, which turned out to be the source, from which it is possible to obtain absolutely any kind of information about absolutely any person. Meaning, information to the smallest particulars and details about what his or her qualities of personality are, how he or she lives, what he or she really wants to achieve, what he or she hides, and much more.

And, it does not matter, if the subject is some person, who lived in the distant past or lives in the present or someone, who will live in the future. Since, as it turned out later on, this literary monument is nothing other than the Catalog of Human Population. In other words, the encyclopedia of *Homo sapiens*; in essence, the same as encyclopedias, reference books for specialists, which contain complete information about representatives of a particular subspecies of animals, plants, etc.

Although at some point, the course of this story turned banal: "bad guys" from security services, intelligence services, politics decided to not only use this source of knowledge for their dirty deeds, but also to appropriate it solely for their personal use. And, the way they tried to do this is also banal: by physically destroying the author of discovery of the Catalog of Human Population and all of his colleagues.

However, the ending of this story makes it stand out from the category of ordinary spy stories. At least because the main characters of this story managed to survive not due to favorable concatenation of circumstances or someone's help, but thanks to that knowledge, which they discovered in the ancient Chinese monument that turned out to be the Catalog of Human

Population. Since, being one of the most ancient sources preserved in this civilization (according to some researchers it dates back to XXIII century BC), this monument contains not only information concerning the structure and functioning of psychophysiology of the entire *Homo sapiens* population, but also unique recipes.

The story of how this survival occurred technically is described in the following sections of this book. It is highly probable that this story might turn out to be informative and somewhat unexpected. Especially for fans of spy stories, who are familiar with activities of security services only from books and movies, which do not describe how things happen in reality. And, the evidence of that this story, despite being fantastic, is not someone's fantasies are official documents, in which it is recorded—declarations from political cases of Andrey Davydov and Olga Skorbatyuk, developers of the Catalog of Human Population. Originals of these documents are stored at the United States Department of Homeland Security, Federal Bureau of Investigation (FBI), etc., and the evidence of this is presented in the Appendix in the form of photos of these documents.

This book is not memoirs and it certainly is not an autobiography, despite that I personally was a direct participant of some events described in this story. I am telling about events from lives of my colleagues in research and I am doing it in the format of a chronicle; that is, without refracting described events through the prism of my personal thoughts, opinions, attitudes, and so on. As the saying goes, only dry facts.

This book does not contain details of personal lives of developers of the Catalog of Human Population—Andrey Davydov and his colleague in scientific research Olga Skorbatyuk. Also, it does not contain a description of their entire life paths, their biographies. This book describes only a limited period of their lives; to be more precise, the period between 2000 and 2011. That what occurred before this period is briefly mentioned in chapters following the Introduction.

This book does not describe that what happened after 2011 and that what is happening right now. Even though the story with persecutions, unfortunately, continues to this day, Andrey Davydov and Olga Skorbatyuk, as well as all staff members of the Special Scientific Info-Analytical Laboratory—Catalog of Human Souls prefer to tell about their scientific research and discoveries, and not about this story or about themselves personally. After all, by its level of captivation and significance, even the most exciting story from people's lives cannot compare with multifarious, often shocking and practically very useful information that researchers obtain from the ancient source of knowledge Shan Hai Jing and other ancient books, which they study.

Readers of this book might be wondering: why does it have such title, if people in this story managed to run away from killers? The reason is that, unfortunately, not everyone managed to survive. People died as a result of persecution by Federal Security Service of Russian Federation. However, mentions of this, stories of how and where it happened, their names and so on cannot be presented in this book due to certain specific reasons. However, this is precisely why the ancient Chinese monument Shan Hai Jing, which turned out to be the Catalog of Human Population, is really a book covered with blood. Blood of innocent people, who were killed because they happened to be in the way of scumbags from Federal Security Service of Russian Federation, who by any means want to take possession of information from the ancient source of knowledge about structure of a human and his psyche, the Catalog of Human Population. And, they want to have this Catalog only for themselves, even though this ancestral heritage must belong to all humanity.

In conclusion, I would like to use this opportunity to state that you will not find names of people, who are somehow connected to this story—not in this book, not anywhere else, for example, in our other books or on the Internet. Their names cannot be disclosed due to confidentiality, which these people want to have, as well as for security purposes.

The main reason for writing this book is that many of those, who learn about the discovery of the Catalog of Human Population want to know about the person, who made this discovery and about his colleagues in scientific activity, but accurate information about all of this was not and still is not available anywhere except this book and the website of the Human Population Academy (http://www.humanpopulationacademy.org).

This occurs for two reasons. The first reason is explained in detail in the Introduction to Book 1 of the Catalog Of Human Souls series and is connected with that all reliable information about us on the Internet almost always gets destroyed; immediately or after some time. The Introduction mentioned above contains some examples of this, even though those are not the only cases. The second reason of that it is impossible to find comprehensive information anywhere (including on the Internet) about the author of scientific discovery of the Catalog of Human Population—Andrey Davydov, about his colleague in developments of this Catalog—Olga Skorbatyuk, about myself, the founder and the director of the Human Population Academy, about all other staff members of the Special Scientific Info-Analytical Laboratory—Catalog Of Human Souls, and about our partners in research and business is confidentiality of all this information. Everything that we are ready to tell about ourselves is presented in this book, as well as on our website at http://www.humanpopulationacademy.org.

Unfortunately, due to confidentiality of personal information and for security reasons, we cannot provide any other information about any one of us. Neither I nor anyone else has the right to provide information about our laboratory's staff and about our partners, to reveal their names, provide their telephone numbers, email addresses, and so on. And, I am officially stating this is this book. This is done so that every person knows that if somewhere in public sources, for example, on the Internet, one comes across statements that someone is an employee of our Laboratory or Academy and his/her name and contact information are provided—it means that this is disinformation or fraud (or both).

It so happened that those people, who use the Catalog of Human Population, and especially those, who are directly related to scientific research of Andrey Davydov and Olga Skorbatyuk have to stay, so to speak, invisible. And, we—authors of the Catalog Of Human Souls book series— truly envy them in this sense. To our great regret, now we simply have nowhere to hide, as we already "became famous," and this happened against our will and against our wishes. However, everyone else who has any relation to the Catalog of Human Population, including our colleagues from the Laboratory and the Academy, between fame, glory, recognition and life have every right to choose the latter. After all, Shan Hai Jing, unfortunately, is a book already covered with blood.

# CHAPTER 1

# "SPY SUPER THRILLER
# FOR HOLLYWOOD"

In 2011 when a translator from one of translation service centers in Los Angeles familiarized himself with contents of declarations to be submitted with the application for political asylum, which were given to him by developers of the Catalog of Human Population Andrey Davydov and Olga Skorbatyuk, who fled from Russia to the United States of America and miraculously survived after Russian security services made repeated attempts to kill them, the only thing he said was: "This is a spy super thriller script for Hollywood!" At that time Hollywood was just a few steps away, but developers of the Catalog of Human Population had other than Hollywood things on their minds, and the text of this "spy super story," bypassing Hollywood directors, went straight to the United States Department of Homeland Security.

The "spy super story" did not end with this. According to Andrey Davydov and Olga Skorbatyuk, the first thing that they saw when they arrived at the U.S. Department of Homeland Security was their lawyer with a suitcase on wheels standing at the entrance to the building. He explained: "I simply could not carry this in my hands." The second thing that amazed Andrey Davydov and Olga Skorbatyuk, as well as all those, who were present during this event, was the volume of documents, which were taken out of this suitcase—they looked like two huge "bricks." They did not at all fit through the window for filing cases, and so an employee of U.S. Department of Homeland Security had to come out and take these "bricks" from the lawyer's hands. These were political cases of developers of the Catalog of Human Population.

In addition to documents that are usually present when applying for political asylum (for example, documents from official sources, testimony from witnesses, medical documents, which confirm facts of persecution), Andrey Davydov's and Olga Skorbatyuk's cases included other kind of materials. They were devoted exclusively to the subject of their research— the Catalog of Human Population. Since the Catalog of Human Population was precisely the reason why a group of employees of Federal Security Service of Russian Federation (FSB, former KGB) at the time headed by the colonel of Foreign Intelligence Service—Andrey Dmitrievich Polonchuk—tried to kill Andrey Davydov and Olga Skorbatyuk.

The subject of Andrey Davydov's and Olga Skorbatyuk's scientific research—the Catalog of Human Population—turned out to be not an easy matter in this difficult political case for employees of U.S. Department Of Homeland Security. However, they had to gain an understanding of this matter because precisely this research was the motive of persecution of developers of the Catalog of Human Population by Russian security services.

These persecutions included systematic attempts to physically destroy developers of the Catalog of Human Population and people directly involved in this research. These attempts were made by abovementioned group of employees of FSB on the territory of Russia for about seven years, and then continued on the territory of the United States of America. For example, in 2013, after an attempted attack on Andrey Davydov and Olga Skorbatyuk was made by a group of three officers of FSB of Russian Federation dressed in civilian clothes when Davydov and Skorbatyuk were walking on the beach in Marina Del Rey (California), they were forced to turn to the Federal Bureau of Investigation (FBI).

The interest of the abovementioned group of FSB officers to the Catalog of Human Population and the desire to have it solely for their own use were so great that judging by certain indicators, persecutions of Andrey Davydov and Olga Skorbatyuk were carried out by a group led by colonel of Foreign Intelligence Service of FSB of Russian Federation A.D. Polonchuk without orders from above; that is, without orders from the director of FSB and the President of Russian Federation (at the time—Dmitry Medvedev). For those, who are familiar with work of security services, this in itself is nonsense since even high-ranking officials of Federal Security Service of Russia under the statute are required to obtain permission from their superiors in order to carry out such operations.

Also, it is possible that this could have happened because the initiator of persecutions of developers of the Catalog of Human Population—colonel of Foreign Intelligence Service of FSB of Russia, Andrey Dmitrievich Polonchuk—was among those, who in 2000 participated in a conspiracy against recently "enthroned" Vladimir Putin (Dmitry Medvedev's predecessor and current President of the Russian Federation).

However, let's get back to events, which occurred on the territory of the United States of America in 2011-2012. At some point, scientific discovery made by Russian researcher, specialist in Chinese culture Andrey Davydov—the Catalog of Human Population—brought employees of U.S. Department Of Homeland Security to an impasse. When Andrey Davydov and Olga Skorbatyuk appeared for an interview for the first time, they waited for several hours, and then they were informed of that their interview is rescheduled for a few days later. And, when they appeared for an interview for the second time, they saw a puzzled face of an officer of U.S. Department of Homeland Security, to whom their cases were transferred.

The first thing that the officer said was: "I apologize that you had to wait, but in our practice we have never come across cases of such volume and complexity. It took me a few days just to read these cases." And then he added: "I hope that you will help me understand the subject of your scientific research, the Catalog of Human Population. It will be difficult for me to look into this case without having an understanding of the essence and significance of this research."

During the interview at the U.S. Department of Homeland Security, developers of the Catalog of Human Population were interviewed in the way that is necessary in such cases: separately, with a qualified interpreter and a second interpreter on the phone line. However, the unusual thing was that during both interviews there was less discussion about persecution of developers of the Catalog by the Federal Security Service of Russia, about attempts to kill them, about politics, and about other matters from the same category than about the subject of scientific research of Andrey Davydov and Olga Skorbatyuk—the Catalog of Human Population. Therefore, each interview lasted many hours.

However, despite that the Catalog of Human Population is not simply an element of this story, but rather its core, it does not make sense to tell about it in detail in this book because general information about it is provided in the Preface and the rest is detailed in previous four books on the Catalog Of Human Souls series. For those, who are not yet familiar with them, the titles of these books are as follows:

- ❖ Book 1. *Homo Sapiens* Are Bio-Robots. Human "Software."
- ❖ Book 2. Hack Anyone's Soul. 100 Demos Of Human Programs From The Catalog Of Human Population.
- ❖ Book 3. Human Manipulation Modes. Either You Are Manipulating Or You Are Being Manipulated.
- ❖ Book 4. Non-Traditional Psychoanalysis. Selected Scientific Articles And Presentations At Conferences.

All of them are published, including in electronic format, and can be read free of charge simply by searching for their titles in Internet search engines. This book is dedicated not to the Catalog of Human Population, but to its main developers—Russian researcher-sinologist Andrey Davydov and his colleagues in research, psychologist Olga Skorbatyuk.

In conclusion, the only thing left to add is that information about the Catalog of Human Population together with other data from political cases of developers of this Catalog was verified by employees of U.S. Department of Homeland Security and other organizations, and on this basis in 2012 Andrey Davydov and Olga Skorbatyuk were granted political asylum in the United States of America. Photos of documents, which confirm this, can be found in the Appendix.

# CHAPTER 2

# STORY FROM POLITICAL CASE OF ANDREY DAVYDOV—THE AUTHOR OF DISCOVERY AND THE MAIN DEVELOPER OF THE CATALOG OF HUMAN POPULATION

### "Declaration

My name is Davydov, Andrey Nikolaevich (Andrey Davydov). I, the undersigned, declare the following to be true and correct to the best of my recollection under penalty of perjury:

## Introduction

1. I was born on March 30th, 1953 in Frunze, Kirghizia of former USSR (Kyrgyzstan). I was raised in Moscow, Russia, attended good schools, have worked hard in my life, and have no criminal history. I have two children. They live in Moscow. My father is deceased. My mother always lives in Moscow. ...

2. My partner, Olga Vladimirovna Skorbatyuk ("Olga"), and I came to the United States on B-2 visas on March 31, 2011. She and I are independently asking for political asylum from the government of the United States, in view of the fact that FSB agents (former KGB) are trying to kill us; and it is being done with the furtive consent of Russian government. (Olga's declaration is included with my application and my declaration is included with her application.)

3. Members of the FSB are trying to eliminate me because I provided compromising materials regarding upper Russian executives to FSB Colonel Andrey Dmitrievich Polonchuk. These materials contained opposition research against Putin to show his vulnerabilities and ability to stay in power; the materials were specifically requested by Colonel Polunchuk in furtherance of an apparent plot within the FSB to overthrow Putin shortly after he came into power. It was said in these materials that former President, current Prime Minister of Russia, Putin was a theoretical and practical mastermind behind terrorist acts in his country and abroad. These

materials also mentioned the volume of financial means, which Putin possessed: where he took it, how he accumulated it, and how he used it. It was said in the handed over materials that Putin's financial fortune was based on the use of FSB as an instrument to take by force financial means of some Russian citizens, who were illegally transferring large amounts of money abroad from Russian Federation. There was talk of very large amounts. These materials contained the information that citizens who were trying to resist Putin's robbery were eliminated with impunity and their money was transferred to Putin's personal accounts abroad.

4. Additionally, over the span of approximately 5 years I provided other materials to Colonel Polunchuk that I now believe were used for nefarious purposes, including internal analysis of the FSB, opposition movements against Putin, and how to get money and from whom.

5. Ultimately, after approximately five years of passing analytical information to Colonel Polonchuk I refused to provide him with further information due to the fact that I was offered to partake in murder. A short time thereafter, I refused to sign the official collaboration agreement with FSB. I did not know at that time that my rejection to work with FSB would automatically trigger my death sentence as one who had information compromising the apparent loyalty of FSB generals and upper Russian executives to Putin as well as evidence of the sinister involvement in various nefarious and criminal activities of members of the FSB.

6. Olga and I suspect members of the FSB are persecuting Olga and me (on account of our scientific research) because we have experienced and suffered strange, unmotivated, and inexplicable health problems since refusing to continue to provide information to the FSB. The suspicious nature of the onset of our symptoms increased when we discovered that the main door to our apartment was broken into; and when our relatives and friends, who visited our place often, started having ailments similar to ours. After contacting experts who examined our apartment, we discovered that our living space (Olga's apartment) contained chemical substances in quantities hazardous for health and life. It was discovered that there were heavy metals in my blood; excesses of lead by 40% and of cadmium by 20%. These discoveries are supported with documents from the official institutions where the studies were performed. The experts' opinions found our apartment inhabitable because of the large quantities of poisonous substances. In short, doctors reported that we got poisoned. The experts from the Federal Center for Hygiene and Epidemiology who conducted the examination of out premises concluded that the poisoning substances which were found were not connected to furniture or renovation. They also made it clear that if these substances were planted there, then it was a professional who did it; perhaps, using special equipment. They said that a non-professional would not be able to do it. The experts justified their

opinion by stating that a person who was not connected to special services of the Russian Federation would have no access to the substances, nor would he or she have the ability to apply them in the manner applied.

7. We know the poisoning was not a simple criminal act or retaliation for any criminal activity because Olga, our relatives, acquaintances, colleagues and I have never committed any criminal actions or participated in any criminal activities. Besides, criminal groups are not capable of the high skill of implementation, which was demonstrated in the attempts to kill us.

8. The manner and methods of the attempts on the lives of Olga and me, such as the sophistication of poisoning mixtures, the unrestricted breaking into the premises, the wiretap of our phones / buildings / cars, the hacking of our computers [which had Linux operating system], and also the complete failure of law-enforcement agencies to protect us are clearly, in my opinion, pointing out that it was the work of FSB or some kind of special forces who kill professionally in Russia and abroad; groups such as the GRU (Central Intelligence Agency) and FSB. I doubt GRU was persecuting us since they didn't have reasons for it. I can't say the same about FSB since I was conducting analytical forecasts for one of the FSB agents from 1999 to 2003.

9. After learning about my scientific research, the FSB colonel Polonchuk asked me to give him information about Putin, who just in May of 2000 came to power. Polonchuk was interested in how long Putin could conceivably remain in power, what kind of personal capital the new President had, how he made it, how he used it and where he kept it. I was quite capable of answering these questions since the subject of my scientific research was the Catalog of Human Population. The Catalog of Human Population was developed based on the decoding of the ancient Chinese manuscript Shan Hai Jing (Classic of the Mountains and Seas).

10. Using the Catalog of Human Population, one can deduce the characteristics of any person and his/her actions by using special estimation methodology which I developed. Specifically important, the Catalog of Human Population can determine vicious or illegal actions which he/she would like to hide from scrutiny. At the request of Colonel Polonchuk, I gave him the abovementioned information about Putin and others (see below). Colonel Polonchuk was not only ordering the information about the former President of the country, but also was a part of the team, which didn't want Putin to be at the power. We believe that Polonchuk had an intention to finish us so Putin could never find out about his attitude, plans, and past actions.

11. It is also possible that Colonel Polonchuk and his FSB colleagues were planning on using the Catalog of Human Population as a powerful tool for theft, all types of violence and murder of those people who opposed the President, Prime Minister and themselves; and for accomplishing other

criminal actions. He gave me several hints that FSB strongly objected to the general public finding out about the existence of this ancient source of knowledge. Since I didn't agree to participate in their criminal riots in the role of analyst and due to the fact that Polonchuk realized during the time of working with me that their analysts were not capable of getting the information about people from Shan Hai Jing or the Catalog of Human Population without my help, Polonchuk decided to act based on the principle: "If not ours, then nobody's!"

## Beginning, Introductions, Verifications, and the FSB's Colonel Polunchuk

12. This story began in Summer 1999. One year before the Russian president Vladimir Vladimirovich Putin came to power, I met Colonel A. D. Polonchuk, who was a SVR colonel (Foreign Intelligence Service, one of the FSB departments). I have to note, however, that I found out Polonchuk was a FSB officer only a year later, in the summer of 2000.

13. In June or July1999 a man called me, and he introduced himself as Andrey Dmitrievich Polonchuk. According to him, he found the information about my scientific research and me in the Moscow magazine Power of Spirit, where I published the article "Shan Hai Jing: Myths or Psyche structure?" in co-authorship with one of my acquaintances from ITAR TASS V. Fedoruk (Russian version of this article http://www.shjlab.com/forum/showthread.php?t=26853. [Note: this article can now be found here: http://www.humanpopulationacademy.org/publications/] At that time I was doing the same thing I do now - I was conducting scientific research and I was decrypting the ancient Chinese manuscript Shan Hai Jing (Classic of the Mountains and Seas), which turned out to be the Catalog of Human Population. Using the Catalog of Human Population methodology which I developed, one can obtain the information from this ancient source about any characteristics of any person, regardless of whether we were acquainted or not, his/her race, nationality, social status and other factors. Moreover, one can obtain such detailed information about any person, knowing only the month, day, year of birth and the gender (place and time of birth are irrelevant). The Catalog of Human Population describes the entire human population which is why it was called the Catalog of Human Population. By the time I met Polonchuk, my technology of decrypting Shan Hai Jing was completed (I began my research in 1975), tested it for 3 years on a sample of approximately 3,000 people, and validated it using the scientific standards point of view.

14. The Catalog's attributes attracted my new acquaintance, Polunchuk to contact me and ask for me information. Shan Hai Jing's decryption not only opens up the possibility of obtaining information about the type of person

one is dealing with and specifically about his/her true essence and hidden motivation mechanisms, but also about his/her actions including those actions, which the person is trying to keep clandestine. In addition, the Catalog offers information about the methods of how to regulate (manipulate) people using untraceable methods of influence without being noticed as such.

15. Polonchuk told me he was very interested in my research and offered to meet me. He also asked me in advance whether I had information about him personally. I obviously responded affirmatively, since "Shan Hai Jing" has information about any person. Then Polonchuk asked me in a very polite manner to bring these materials to the meeting.

16. Several days later we met not far from MHAT theatre, at the boulevard. I brought the information which Polonchuk requested, a decoding of his individual program from the Catalog in the form of express analysis. Polonchuk reviewed the documents I gave him and he was very impressed with the materials. According to him, he saw himself in the description. We parted ways after this.

17. Polonchuk was organizing our further meetings over the phone. We were meeting in different cafes and restaurants including café Pyramid near the movie theatre Pushkin at the Pushkin Square, a Chinese restaurant at the new MHAT building, and a café near the metro stop Ohotnyj Ryad.

18. At first, Polunchuk exclusively requested personal information from the Catalog: about his relatives, son, wife and acquaintances. He justified his requests stating that he had to be certain that the technology of estimating the structure of human psyche and decryptions of human programs from the ancient text Shan Hai Jing were really working. I never objected to his requests for verification of my theory and gave him all the information he was requesting.

19. This verification process lasted almost a year and included reviews into various subjects known to Polunchuk so he could compare my findings with his own understanding of the subjects. At the end of the verification process, Polonchuk announced that he had no objections or complaints in regards to received information. And only then, in the summer of 2000, during one of our meetings, he introduced himself as an FSB agent and showed his identification as a Colonel in the Foreign Intelligence Service. During the same meeting, Polonchuk asked me to prepare analytical materials about V.V. Putin, who recently (in May of 2000) came to power. The goals of this analysis were the following: find out if the new Russian President was temporary or not, how long Putin would stay at power, which personal financial capital he had, where he kept it and how he used it.

20. I didn't have any problems with answering these questions; I could obtain all the information about the new Russian President, which

Polonchuk was interested in, using the Catalog. The analytical work he requested regarding Putin was beyond the depth of any analysis I had conducted previously, which is why as a researcher I found the request rather interesting. In addition, the work paid well. (As a note, in the year 2000 the average salary of Russian citizens was approximately the equivalent of $83 per month, and I got offered the equivalent of $...,000 for this work). I was exclusively conducting scientific research at that time and I didn't have stable income and I needed money, so I couldn't miss this opportunity. Most importantly though, when I agreed to this offer, I didn't know that all the analysts who were conducting similar forecasts for FSB didn't live for long. And people who had compromising information about FSB generals and colonels (in this case I had information that Polonchuk, his management, and colleagues were part of an anti-Putin group) were eliminated even faster. (Obviously if I knew then what I know now about the manner and methods of FSB work, I would have halted my communication with Polonchuk regardless of the pay.)

21. I completed my work and gave the materials about Putin to Polonchuk and Polunchuk handed me the agreed-upon fee. Polonchuk was disappointed in the results of this research: his bosses, a group of his colleagues from FSB and him were hoping that Putin would not remain in power for long and that Putin would be replaced in one to two months. This group, most probably, counted on becoming loyal to a new leader, one who conceivably would replace the new President. (Polonchuk never openly stated that he was against Putin, but his actions and his indirect discussion made his loyalty clear to me). The research into Putin's personality pointed out that the anti-Putin hopes had no chance of realizing. My analysis clearly indicated that Putin not only would occupy the President's chair for long, but that he was also planning on building a power system, which would cover the entire Eurasian region. My findings also showed that Putin would be able to find financial means for this global project through his use of the FSB (as the repressive apparatus to illegally take money from people who were transferring their capitals abroad or accumulating it within the Russian Federation).

22. Although I believe that I upset Polonchuk with my predictions about Putin, he later enthusiastically thanked me for my analytical work, gave me a bonus in the amount of $ ...,000 and explained the bonus by stating that I seriously helped him and his bosses by calculating who Putin was and what kind of policy he would implement. He said that because of my analytical work, this FSB group was not only not fired, but also through knowing Putin's characteristics they were able to position themselves to advance in their careers. However, I was still really surprised about this generous bonus. On one hand it was quite logical, yet on the other hand it wasn't typical for FSB to be generous with money, as I had noticed over our past several transactions.

23. It is necessary to note that money and research curiosity were not the basic reason to my agreement to fulfilling orders from Polonchuk. My main reason for agreeing to work with Polunchuk was that I hoped the relationship would lead to large investments from the government for a new laboratory for my research. Polonchuk and I discussed the possibility of additional funding, he did not say exactly where the money would come from but he did say that he and his organization for very interested in having the Catalog at their disposal through their own laboratory, and I thought it would mean more funding for me to perform broader research, the creation of a laboratory that I would run, and which would attract different specialists that would assist me to expedite the process of creating the complete version of the Catalog. The personnel ad financing at the already existing laboratory, the laboratory "Totems" founded by Andrey Vladimirovich Varfalomeev, was insufficient for the level of research necessary to complete the Catalog. I believed that the Catalog of Human Population was so important to the Russian people and the entire world that it needed to be completed on a governmental scale with government assistance and Polonchuk agreed with my opinion. In fact, during one of our conversations, Polonchuk expressed his interest in financing the advancement of the project of creating the complete version of the Catalog of Human Population. His interest persuaded me to work as an analyst, fulfilling unofficial orders from FSB. I knew the FSB and Russian special services had large personal monetary funds, not to mention many connections they had in different social layers, so I was convinced that they would fund my research if I kept working with them.

24. Although he showed interest and kept telling me that the Catalog of Human Population would receive the financing I sought, month after month, Polonchuk prolonged the decision regarding the financing of my laboratory. He often told me that we would talk specifics about the financing and the new laboratory "tomorrow" or "next time we meet" and would offer me additional analytical work projects for me to do for his agency while the financing and laboratory logistics were being worked out. I continued to agree to the projects in order not to loose the opportunity to for the Catalog of Human Population that Polunchuk and I had discussed, and also because I needed the financial assistance that projects provided for me.

25. Polonchuk's meetings with me were characterized by long breaks. Polonchuk would usually disappear for 2-6 months followed by a call to schedule a meeting. I did not call him because he had multiple phones and changed his numbers regularly.

26. With the hope that Polonchuk would soon redeem his promise in regards to the laboratory, I fulfilled a series of orders. Unfortunately, given that it's been 11 years, I can't remember the exact time and dates of one or

another order. I also, unfortunately, can't name all those people who Polonchuk introduced me to since they never gave me their full names while placing a direct order. All I knew was that they were Polonchuk's colleagues at FSB. Polonchuk never gave me their names or job positions. I did not insist on such information though because I was never interested in FSB affairs.

27. I fulfilled a series of orders for Polonchuk. For example, I completed the order for the Antiterrorist Center, where Polonchuk worked at that time. This center's organization was Putin's idea and it was located in Moscow at Old Square. I was asked to complete the theoretical and practical parts on the subject of "Terrorism." So, I did it. I handed over all the materials to Polonchuk in his apartment; he lived around the subway station "Novoslobodskaya." Polonchuk deleted all the analytical materials I had prepared on my computer. (However, I managed to save one of the documents titled "Terrorism Concepts," confirming my authorship in these developments.) I also completed a few other orders. I handed over analytical materials about the owner of the weaving factory in the city of Ivanovo and the governor of the Primorye Territory. I also developed the election campaign strategy for the future governor of Moscow district and President of the republic of Sakha (Yakutia).

## Refusing Further Assistance to the FSB, Meeting Olga, and Poor Health

28. My business relations with Polonchuk became worse at the beginning of summer of 2003. It happened after I refused to conduct research on one Canadian businessman who was selling dental equipment. Polonchuk wanted my research on the man to help him with his own task, which was to recruit this businessman to spy for the FSB, or if he refused to help the FSB, then to illegally take his money and or eliminate him. I refused to work on the project involving the Canadian businessman because I did not want to participate, even indirectly, in murdering people. Polonchuk reacted so negatively to my rejection that it provoked in him almost an open reaction of anger.

29. Two or three months after I refused to give Polunchuk information about the Canadian, then being summer 2003, Polonchuk called me and offered to meet in one of the usual places, the café Pyramid. There, Polonchuk asked me to sign documents attesting to my official collaboration with FSB. The documents did not contain specific dates regarding the collaboration, but I was led to understand that by signing the documents I would be expected to help the FSB as long as I was alive. I strongly declined to sign the documents. Polonchuk left even angrier than last time when I had refused to help with the Canadian businessman. This turned out to be our last meeting.

30. The end of summer 2003 was also the first time that I became seriously ill: I felt tired all the time and I had strange pain in my left leg. However, I was perfectly healthy prior to these ailments. I could not maintain my normal and active lifestyle and I could not continue my work on the Catalog of Human Population either. I was bedridden all the time due to my constant fatigue and my left leg was hurting so much that I had to bandage it in order to be able to sleep. The conditioned worsened from limping to barely being able to move to not being able to walk at all.

31. In November 2003 I met Olga Skorbatyuk, my future common law wife and partner in scientific research work on the Catalog of Human Population. She is a professional psychologist and she was referred to me by our common acquaintance <name>. Olga contacted me to obtain information about herself and a few of her colleagues.

32. I gave Olga and her colleagues this information in the form of decrypted programs; although it took me much longer to complete this work due to my bad health. Olga and her colleagues were impressed with the materials and told me the descriptions depicted them, their personal qualities, and their life algorithms exactly. They also told me they were surprised that the information they received was true, exact and complete.

33. After confirming the existence and accuracy of the Catalog of Human Population for herself and with other psychologists, Olga expressed her interest in participating in my research at the beginning of 2004. I agreed to it.

34. At the same time – the end of winter, beginning of spring of 2004 – Olga and I started a personal relationship.

35. Olga began directly participating in the creation of human programs' decryptions from Shan Hai Jing. After feeling exhausted from all the ailments (general weakness and terrible pain in my legs, which began in 2003), Olga's assistance came as welcome relief. Although Olga did not engage in the process of decoding the programs because she did not know how to do the actual decoding, it was still much easier for me to perform my work of decoding by working together.

36. However, our work was not as efficient as we would have liked due to my ailments. Olga told me to seek medical help. I resisted at first since I was not used to having problems with my health or visiting doctors about such things. In the past, I had always fixed all my past minor ailments myself, but these conditions were too much for me. The Catalog of Human Population had helped me to understand my path, a path of health and until this period in my life, I was healthy.

37. However, when my health did not improve on its own and in turn interrupted my research on the Catalog of Human Population, I agreed to Olga's persuasion. Thus, on August 19, 2004, I underwent a medical

examination at the Outpatient Clinic at the Department of Defense in Moscow. The examination results terrified me: computer tomography showed that I had a delaminating abdominal aortic aneurysm. Due to the mortal danger, I was recommended to undergo an urgent surgery.

38. Out of the blue, Polonchuk called me not long before my hospitalization. He wanted to schedule another meeting to place another order. However, despite the fact that my upcoming surgery was very expensive and I was looking for financial means in order to be able to afford it, I declined to meet with him about the order. I did not want to have anything in common with this sleazy and dishonorable man whose personal qualities I detested. (I would like to note that even after this incident, Polonchuk was regularly (every 4-6 months) calling me during the period of 2004-2010 in order to get what he wanted, i.e. he was insisting on getting analytical materials for yet another candidate. Every time I would politely refuse, using different excuses. In response to my rejection, Polonchuk would get irritated and angry.)

39. In 2004, they performed aortic bypass surgery and placed a stent in my body. The reason for delaminating abdominal aortic aneurysm remained unknown. (Later, when reading one of the articles about the effect of poisoning substances on the human body, Olga and I accidentally found the information that one of the consequences could be a delaminating abdominal aortic aneurysm, however, I am unable to find the link to this article right now).

40. Beginning in the second half of 2004 and the entire 2005, due to my severe surgery, we were forced to stop working on the complete version of the Catalog of Human Population. At that time, out of 293 human programs, described in Shan Hai Jing, no more than 50 were decoded.

41. However, as soon as I started feeling better, I asked Olga to write a series of scientific articles to educate the public and the scientific community about the Catalog of Human Population. Together, we created a series of articles such as: From Carl Gustav Jung's archetypes of the collective unconscious to individual archetypical patterns, Archetype Semantics: how it relates to the notion of 'Image', How archetypical are Images?, Could archetypal images have Chimera depiction?, and Society as manipulating and manipulated community. (The Russian version of these articles is available at http://www.shjlab.com/content/blogsection/19/106/lang,ru/, but unfortunately only one article out of the above has been translated to English so far http://shjlab.com/content/blogsection/19/106/lang,en/). [Note: these articles are now available at http://www.humanpopulationacademy.org/hpa-press-publishing/]

42. We were planning on including all of these articles as chapters in the upcoming book Manual of non-traditional psychoanalysis. The existence of

these articles formed the factual beginning of yet another scientific direction in psychology, which was based on the decryption of Shan Hai Jing. All of these articles have copyright under the Russian Community of Author's Rights.

43. After writing these articles, Olga and I made the decision in 2005 to write and publish a series of books, in which we presented the possibilities of our technology. The articles were written using strict scientific language, but we also wanted the information to be available to the general public so that anybody could read about the Catalog. So, we created these books for the general public. There were four books and they covered the following groups of people: (1) people born on April 5th leap years and April 6th common years, (2) people born on March 22nd leap years and March 23rd common years, (3) people born on December 6th leap years and December 7th common years, and (4) people born October 12th leap years and October 13th common years. These books were written using popular science language and they as a series were titled Manipulative Games for Women.

44. My recovery was very slow, so after we published these books in the fall of 2005, Olga took the lead in distributing the information about the discovery of the Catalog of Human Population. We created the website "The Catalog of Human Population" (http://shjlab.com), where anybody could get information in order to test the possibilities of the technology we had. We still had not decrypted that many human programs from the Collection of Mountains and Seas, however, there were enough of them, from our point of view, to give an idea to people as to what we offered. The test was simple and didn't require any special means or special education. After reviewing a short video (in Russian language in the section "Demos" (on the left) -
http://shjlab.com/component/option,com_frontpage/Itemid,1/lang,ru/' In English, in the section "Demo: programs of homo" (on the left) http://shjlab.com/component/option,com_frontpage/Itemid,1/lang,en/),
anybody who was interested could compare the descriptions which were offered with what they knew about real people. [Note: demos are now available at http://www.humanpopulationacademy.org/human-programs-demo/] If somebody did not have any acquaintances with birthdates matching those in the videos, they, as we thought, could find these people on the Internet without any difficulties and could verify the accuracy of our understanding of this ancient book.

45. Also, at the beginning of Fall 2005, Olga offered information about the Catalog's discovery to various media. In October 2005, she was invited on a TV show. Olga appeared on the Moscow TV channel TDK. She appeared in a series of TV shows dedicated to our scientific work. [Note: recordings are now available at http://www.humanpopulationacademy.org/olga-

skorbatyuk-russian-television] The shows were extensive, lasted approximately one hour each, ran live, and gave Olga a forum to talk theory and give examples of descriptions or programs from the Catalog of Human Population.

46. According to the editor of the show, the specific episodes in which Olga appeared had a very high rating among viewers and our topic received a hearty response from viewers. The live broadcasts always received lots of phone calls. People, who were rather surprised with and puzzled by the similarity of our presented descriptions, asked questions and shared their opinions. The most important fact was that nobody who called said the information was wrong or incomplete. All Olga's appearances on TV can be found at the main page of the Russian version of our website, right column http://shjlab.com/component/option,com_frontpage/Itemid,1/lang,ru/). [Note: recordings are now available at http://www.humanpopulationacademy.org/olga-skorbatyuk-russian-television] People who called the show actually confirmed that everything that Olga shared during these live broadcasts was accurate about them. In December of 2005, she appeared on another TV channel of Moscow – "Capital."

47. However, despite viewers' clear interest towards Olga's presentations on the Catalog of Human Population and their increasing popularity, the scheduled live broadcast with Olga's participation on March 23, 2006 was blocked from going on the air and her next slated appearance scheduled for April 6, 2006 was cancelled even though all the materials for that show were already prepared. The TV editors did not or could not give a clear explanation as to why it happened. From a business standpoint, it made no sense because the shows with Olga were good for business. The shows with Olga were also very popular so it made no sense that they would choose not to air the program on March 23 or cancel the April 6th show. The editors tried to come up with some reasons but they were not convincing.

48. A little bit later, in the summer of 2006, bookstores started giving us our books back; and again, it was despite buyers' clear interest towards them. The returns and cancellations were coupled with the same flawed unconvincing explanations Olga had to listen to from TDK as to why they stopped the TV project.

49. I already suspected, of course, who could be in our way of distributing the information about the Catalog of Human Population. The Special Services of the Russian Federation monitor all information broadcasted in the media and on the Internet. I had my own history of communicating with FSB and had refused to continue to use the Catalog of Human Population toward their malignant ends so it made sense that they would try to stop us from sharing the Catalog of Human Population with anyone else, much less the general public. However, at that time we did not think

that my refusal to continue to work on projects and complete orders for the FSB was so serious that our death sentences were already signed, and that we were already slowly being killed by poisons.

50. Beginning October 2005, right after Olga's first appearance on TV, people started contacting us through our website. People were asking for information from the Catalog of Human Population about themselves, their relatives, and acquaintances. These were regular Russian citizens and also citizens of other former Soviet Union countries (Ukraine, Byelorussia, Baltic). Russian speaking residents of Europe and America were also contacting us. They found out about us through TV shows, our books and Internet.

51. By that time I started feeling significantly better and I returned to the decoding of Shan Hai Jing. These people were offering their sponsorship in exchange for information. Since we were always finding our own financial means to support our research (thanks to the fact that the information from the Catalog of Human Population has vast practical application), we were happy to help people and make some money. Soon, we had a big line of people, who requested the information and we worked a lot. We finally got some money after my prolonged sickness and we were able to pay off our debts.

52. I was particularly pleased since people, who ordered our materials, started giving us their grateful feedback. They were writing to us that, finally, thanks to the discovery of the Catalog of Human Population, they got the opportunity to live a full, normal, happy, and most importantly, theirs, as opposed to somebody else's, life; that they found mutual understanding with those who they were willing to be with, that they built relationships, acquired true freedom, independence, self-confidence, health, and many other things. I was happy that, finally, the Catalog of Human Population found its direct application: it was used for people's good, for their development, for self-perfection, for solving problems. I was also happy that the Catalog was being used not by well-fed State Duma deputies or officials, as it was in the past, not by members of Special Services or by politicians for their dirty affairs, but instead by common people for common good.

53. However, this didn't last for long. Since the summer of 2006, in addition to the problems with TV and books, we started having new problems. Somebody tried to destroy our website. Then we had problems with our bank accounts. We also had problems with internet connection: for example, emails did not reach us or they would disappear; and incoming phone calls would randomly drop or be blocked.

54. The media as well as academic and scientific circles communicated with us with reluctance. On various pretexts, Olga was never invited to appear on TV again despite her offers. We also could not reach an agreement with

periodicals: they would not publish the texts about our research. (The sequence of events was the same: sincere interest at the beginning and then denial.) For example, the magazine Questions of Psychology did not accept Olga's article for publication even though we did not have problems with publishing in that magazine previously. For example, previously my articles about the Catalog of Human Population were regularly published in Moscow magazines such as Oracle, The Spirit Power, and others. In the recent past, I had also communicated often and without hesitation with scientists from different fields of study and not only with the scientists from institutions where I worked. My colleagues in scientific work used to respond with great interest to the information about the Catalog of Human Population. Among them was, for example, doctor of historical sciences, famous sinologist and translator from Chinese language Vladimir Vyacheslavovich Malyavin (http://ru.wikipedia.org/wiki/%D0%9C%D0%B0%D0%BB%D1%8F%D0%B2%D0%B8%D0%BD,_%D0%92%D0%BB%D0%B0%D0%B4%D0%B8%D0%BC%D0%B8%D1%80_%D0%92%D1%8F%D1%87%D0%B5%D1%81%D0%BB%D0%B0%D0%B2%D0%BE%D0%B2%D0%B8%D1%87; as well as another famous sinologist, scientist-orientalist, professor Anatoliy Evgenievich Lukyanov (http://ru.wikipedia.org/wiki/%D0%9B%D1%83%D0%BA%D1%8C%D1%8F%D0%BD%D0%BE%D0%B2,_%D0%90%D0%BD%D0%B0%D1%82%D0%BE%D0%BB%D0%B8%D0%B9_%D0%95%D0%B2%D0%B3%D0%B5%D0%BD%D1%8C%D0%B5%D0%B2%D0%B8%D1%87) and others. The change in communication was obvious and upsetting. No one prevented me in my attempts to talk about my discovery earlier. Instead, earlier I was invited to speak at scientific conferences and round-tables when I worked at International Academy of Anthropology. For example, in 1997, there was First Russian Philosophical Congress "Human Being-Philosophy-Humanism" (Volume VII, The philosophy of human problems, edited by corresponding member RAO Verbickaya, L.A and by associate professor Sokolova B.G., Saint-Petersburg, 1997). [The text of this presentation is available here: in Russian - http://www.humanpopulationacademy.org/publications/ and in English - http://www.humanpopulationacademy.org/courses/shan-hai-jing-original-catalog-of-psychophysical-human-structure/] In 2002, I also presented another one of my papers about the discovery of the Catalog of Human Population at an international conference called the International Conference of Prospects of Preservation and Development of Uniform Planetary Civilization. Culture, Ecology, Cosmos, in Moscow during 2002. [The text of this presentation is available here: in Russian - http://www.humanpopulationacademy.org/publications/ and in English - http://www.humanpopulationacademy.org/courses/catalog-of-human-population/] ...

55. Olga was also frustrated by the mounting rejections and perplexed at how things could have changed so fast for us within the scientific community and in our relation with the media. In 2006 Olga contacted various scientific circles with the hopes of expanding the community's understanding of the Catalog of Human Population. For example, she investigated the possibility of writing her candidate's and doctoral dissertations on the topic of the "Catalog of Human Population." Although her proposal was first met with great interest but was ultimately rejected. In the end, Olga never had the opportunity defend her thesis on the subject.

56. The only thing Olga was able to do in Moscow academic circles was to conduct a series of lectures about the Catalog of Human Population in the II Moscow Medical Institute with the aid of one of her acquaintances, epidemiologist <name>, who taught there and who gave her access on an unofficial basis to his student audience. Similar attempts in other scientific institutions in Moscow were met by uniform denial.

57. We also tried to contact scientists from other countries. We emailed them; however, we didn't receive any responses. I suppose, at that time it was pointless to do so because FSB was monitoring all our mailboxes and such information could not pass through their "filters."

58. We learned that someone was monitoring all our email. Olga discovered that someone broke into her Gmail mailbox. In "settings" she saw the electronic address of someone unknown to us. It turned out that all correspondence, which was addressed to us, was redirected to this unknown person. Someone was monitoring our mailbox. We were unable to find out how long it was going on and who was receiving all our correspondence.

59. In 2006 we also started having problems with our Internet project. No matter where comments about the discovery of the Catalog of Human Population would appear, someone would instantly show up and would start defaming it in a rough and rude manner. Quite often, we or others who were announcing our discovery (and there were more and more people who would do that), would get blocked on forums and the information about the Catalog of Human Population would get deleted. We could not understand why they had this same strange negative reaction and to what it was connected.

60. Later and in what appeared orchestrated, a strange group of guests appeared on our forum (http://www.shjlab.com/forum/) [Note: this website no longer exists; our new website is http://www.humanpopulationacademy.org] and they were systematically insulting Olga and I and all those people who were ordering materials from us. Eventually, the forum administrator blocked these "guests." (Recently, we found an article called Virtual Eye of the Big Brother, which describes how the FSB wages campaigns within Russian Internet forums against

certain sites found to be anti-Putin or subversive in any way (http://www.vestnik.com/issues/2003/0430/win/polyanskaya_krivov_lo mko.htm). Olga and I instantly recognized the familiar style: open rudeness, insults, threats, breaking into mailboxes etc. After the infestation by the group, we were forced to close our forum because the administrator complained that someone tried to break into it and the administrator became scared and was unwilling to put place himself at risk so he quit working as an administrator. He was not the first of the last of our acquaintances to distant himself from us and chooses not to work with us anymore.

61. However, even after we closed the Internet forum on our website, we believe these same unknown people or persons did not stop terrorizing us. People or a single person started bothering our sponsoring clients with phone calls and strange letters. Nobody could understand how these people were able to obtain the emails and phone numbers of our sponsoring clients, especially because everyone knew that the laboratory was protecting the confidentiality of those who contacted us.

62. The same stranger(s) started writing to Olga and I in the same insulting manner as they had written to our sponsors. He, she or they wanted to obtain the materials from the Catalog of Human Population and literally demanded the information. The requests were done in such a rude manner, that we flatly refused to give them information from the Catalog of Human Population. We decided that it would be better for us to lose money than communicate with them.

63. The communications, website attacks, email monitoring, etc., were not the end of this story. One night before we started living together, unfortunately I do not remember the exact date, Olga called me (prior to July 2009 we lived separately). She sounded frightened and nervous. She told me that while she was working, she heard the doorbell ringing. She saw a person [his name and names of other suspected employees of FSB from A. D. Polonchuk's group are provided after the text (under endnote [1])] through the peephole, who told her that he was the one, who got blocked on the forum and that he was demanding the access to the information from the Catalog of Human Population. Olga refused to talk to him. Then, he started banging on the door, while shouting out insults. Olga did not call the police at that time, since her metal door was very durable; in addition, she had more important things to do – she was working on another order from a client.

64. This incident, of course, was not the only one when somebody tried to distract us from our work or interfere with the completion of the Catalog.

65. Approximately at the same time (the end of 2006), Olga started having problems with her health as well. Fatigue, headaches and stomachaches were bothering her, and preventing from doing her work. She started

having a fever every day 37.2-37.4 Celsius (98.96-99.32F). It was very difficult for her to conduct research. Having confirmed that this fever was not connected to any inflammation, colds and so on, she decided to see a doctor. Doctors conducted a complete medical checkup, yet they were unable to identify the reason for the daily sub febrile fever.

66. Around that same time I started feeling bad again too. However, at that time we did not know that Russian special services were poisoning us and we believed our ailments were the result of overworking although some disorders, my sudden chronic rhinitis for example, were not connected to overwork fatigue.

67. In 2007, Olga and I were still working on decoding programs to create the complete version of the Catalog of Human Population, but we started thinking about a much needed and much deserved break. Coincidentally at the end of 2008, an American of Russian origin contacted us and requested the materials about herself. She further invited us to the United States because she was interested in further communication with us and we agreed to her offer.

68. The American, Kate Bazilevsky, who lives in San Diego, California, first ordered the materials about her boyfriend and then about herself. According to her, all the information we provided to her was true. While the accuracy did not surprise Olga or me because we had been doing this work for many people and all of those people had the same reaction, Kate was particularly surprised and impressed because we lived on different continents and had never met her or her boyfriend in person. Being impressed with the possibilities of the Catalog, Kate told her close friend <name> about it. <Name> remained skeptical for a long time regarding the ability of the Catalog. However, one day she decided to try it and contacted us to get the information about her. The day after she received the decoding of one of the manipulation modes of her sub-type structure, <name> decided to get the rest of the materials for her.

69. In 2009 we entered into more constant communication with Kate Bazilevsky. We corresponded regularly and talked over Skype. Kate told us all about San Diego. She lived in Ocean Beach, San Diego and described it as a vacation destination. Olga and I thought Kate's place might be good for us in terms of restoring our health.

70. In July 2009 I moved in with Olga into her apartment. Prior to that, I was regularly visiting her for several days at a time, but we maintained separate apartments.

71. Our health was not improving, but was instead getting worse and worse. For example, in the summer of 2009, they discovered a cyst in my jaw. A cyst had been found previously in Olga's ovary. Although one can consider

the two cysts to be a coincidence, medical sources insist that the effect of poisoning substances can lead, among other things, to cyst formation.

72. Kate Bazilevsky had attempted to persuade us for a long time to visit her and she sent us an invitation. Olga applied for an American tourist visa first which she received in September 2009.

73. In October 2009, she came to the United States for two weeks alone. She went alone because we were planning a prolonged vacation, but wanted to confirm that the location where Kate was inviting us to was suitable for restoring our health. Olga stayed with Kate in San Diego for two weeks in October/November of 2009. Olga, Kate and <name> had a great time together traveling around sightseeing. Olga came back to Moscow delighted with her visit. Based on how pleased she was with her short trip, we made the decision to go to San Diego for our vacation.

74. In January 2010, I got a two-year tourist visa in the embassy of the United States in Moscow. On February 2, 2010, we came to America together. Kate invited us to live with her at ...

75. We didn't make a mistake in our estimations – a half-year vacation from February 2010 to August 2010 really helped us. However, both of us were sick for the first 2-3 months. We did not suspect at that time that our suitcases with all the clothing could have been or had been poisoned at the Russian airport, but looking back it is the only conceivable reason we would be so sick. For example, both of us had a severe cold for one and a half months. For the first time in my life I had pain in my ears and Olga had an unusual skin rash and pink scabs that would burst out, fester and refuse to heal for long periods of time. However, despite all of the initial sickness, by the end of the fourth month in the United States we were swimming, biking and practicing Wushu every day, and we were even playing tennis almost every day.

76. On August 2, 2010, Olga and I returned to Moscow from San Diego. As soon as we came back, we started feeling bad again, although we rationalized that our sickness was the result of re-acclimatization. However, we still had not recovered and no longer believed that our sickness was on account of re-acclimatization. Despite a wonderful and prolonged vacation along the shores of the Pacific Ocean and the good health we had begun to enjoy by the date of our departure from the United States, we felt bad again. All our disorders came back.

77. At some point, complaining to each other again about our ailments, we discovered with surprise that we had the same symptoms. For example, we both felt really weak, incredibly sleepy (we could sleep up to 18 hours per day at that time), strange spasms in the entire body, constant dryness in the mouth, constant heaviness in the chest, periodical nausea, bloating, pain after each food intake, etc. Having noticed the big difference in our health

condition after our return to our homeland, we suspected that something was wrong, something sinister and malignant.

78. At the end of November of 2010, our health became really bad. In addition to abovementioned symptoms, our sight significantly decreased (Olga was unable to focus). We also had problems with breathing, heartbeat, and finger tremors. My thumb numbed from time to time. We both had bitterness in our mouths and we had problems with our skin. These skin problems somewhat resembled the pink spots Olga had on her face in San Diego; however, now we both had them on our faces, arms, and legs (we have pictures). I also suffered from skin boils on her arms, legs, and private parts. We also had disorders with our coordination of movement, and Olga even suffered impairment in her speech. Our memory and thinking functions declined significantly. We could not concentrate. In addition to this, both of us had extremely dry skin, our hair started falling out, and our nails became brittle and broke. My nails started folding inside in a strange manner.

79. The scariest and most alarming of the multiple health problems we had begun to experience since coming back to our apartment in Moscow occurred in November 2010 when I for the first time in my life started having suffocation fits. The first time it happened at night while I was sleeping. I woke up because I could not breathe. I jumped out of bed and ran to the kitchen. I took ice from the freezer, placed it on my throat, and sat next to the fan. I believe that if I had not acted so fast I would have suffocated because the spasm that squeezed my throat shut was very strong and like nothing I had ever experienced before that night.

80. We decided to see a doctor after that fit. On December 1, 2010, Doctor <name>, from the outpatient clinic Aerolife, after hearing about our symptoms (we came to see her together) suspected that both of us had been poisoned. She ran laboratory tests. One of the indices of my blood analysis (extremely high level of the choline esterase) confirmed the doctor's opinion. (As we found out later from the comprehensive medical summaries, the change in the choline esterase level could be connected to the poisoning from the organophosphorous compounds used in weaponized chemicals). The doctor suggested we see a toxicologist. On December 12th, 2010, she gave us referrals.

81. We spent the rest of the month trying to get a consultation with a toxicologist. However, nobody wanted to see us which made no sense to me at the time because we were willing pay for help. We managed to meet with a few medical professionals but the results were not helpful. At the Sklifosofsky Institute, we were prescribed an enema and activated carbon. They did not tell us what to do with the suffocation fits, what kind of poisoning we had, or how to treat it. One doctor who specialized in toxicology heard our story of possible poisoning and then openly humiliated

us, advising us to see a psychiatrist. Another toxicologist, after listening to our complaints declared that these symptoms confused him so much that he was unable to determine what we were poisoned with.

82. Therefore, at the end of December 2010 we did not yet have official documented proof, which would support poisoning. We got it only in January 2011.

83. There are only a few toxicologists in Moscow whom the general public might see and we went to all of them without success at getting lab results about what was happening to us and what poisons were in our systems. We could not understand why they were refusing to treat us. Later, we found an answer to this question. In conversation with one of her acquaintance, a prominent doctor, Olga found out that when any toxicologist ran into a non-traditional case of chronic poisoning symptoms, which were not connected to a job at some hazardous manufacturing plant or to participation in the act of war, he/she preferred not to deal with such a patient. Olga asked why that was so, he told her that doctors tried to escape getting wrapped up into "dark stories." Olga asked what exactly he was talking about and the therapist stated that doctors considered it a most likely assumption that when it was unclear as to who poisoned these patients and with what substances, the poisoners were either connected to criminal groups or Russian Special Services. In addition, he explained that toxicologists treat acute poisoning and or chronic toxic exposure at some manufacturing plant. Since it was evident that we had been poisoned but unclear as to by whom or where, none of the toxicologists wanted to help us or treat us.

84. At the end of December 2010, Olga and I felt we would not be able to get any medical help in Moscow or even anywhere in the Russian Federation. My fits not only continued, but even became stronger. They started happening on an everyday basis, they were really strong and they were life threatening, one of them could become the last. We had to do something. We started looking for information on poisoning substances and poisoning treatment methodologies on our own, reviewing toxicology reference books, scientific articles and any information on the Internet. We studied a huge volume of special literature. The methods we found did not solve the problem with suffocation fits, but at least it all helped us to feel a little better. For example, we started taking calcium chloride several times a day, glucose, Meksidol pills, magnesium sulfate (inside and adding it to baths), and certain essential oils.

85. At the same time we examined all the probable areas in our apartment, where these poisonous substances could be placed. What I could wash, I washed right away (curtains, pillows, blankets, sheets, clothing). In addition, Olga thoroughly cleaned the entire living premises using special cleaning devices, which we read about in special literature, such as

ammonia. We removed the woolen carpet from the room, which had a strange smell despite the fact we dry-cleaned it after we came back from the United States. We wrapped it up in tight bags and put it on the balcony for further expert examination. Later we threw away our sofa, our bed mattress, merino blanket and other things we could not wash at home.

86. Having lost or throw out much of our possessions, we slept on stiff boards and, after we threw away our bed as well, we slept on the floor. However, after all these actions, we started feeling better. Our improvement reassured us that our hypothesis that someone was poisoning us had basis.

87. Our hypothesis was also confirmed on December 31st, 2010, when Olga went outside to take out the garbage and a piece of the lock on the metal front door fell off. Olga picked up the piece that fell off and discovered that it was the metal plate, which covered a portion of the lock. She asked me for help and I tried to fix the lock but discovered that the lock itself was broken too. We also discovered big cracks on each side of the lock, which clearly did not appear on their own. The broken lock completed the picture: somebody broke into our apartment and planted poisonous substances. Only FSB agents could do something like that.

88. I still did not want to believe my suspicions that the FSB were poisoning us so in order to support or reject my suspicions, Olga and I started looking for similar cases in different sources. Through our research it became absolutely clear: anybody who was connected to compiling information against V.V. Putin were killed, poisoned or else disappeared without any trace. We found information that Putin's preferred method of eliminating people who were out of his favor was having the Russian Special Services poison in such a way as to make the death appear to be from natural causes such as pulmonary or brain edema, heart attack, stroke or any other "common" disease. We clearly believed Putin's preferred method was applied to us by the FSB. The FSB was one of the few organizations in Russia, which did not obey government laws, but obeyed only the laws of former Russian President V.V. Putin, like a mafia alliance. The FSB, the former KGB, is nothing else but a legalized group of criminals. The FSB only serves "His Great Majesty" Putin, not the Russian people.

89. In his article Russia's Putin Is A Killer, Timothy Naegele fairly classifies Putin in his article as a dictator and killer. (http://naegeleblog.wordpress.com/2010/02/09/russias-putin-is-a-killer/). Naegele is right. Putin is as sinister and evil as Joseph Stalin, Adolf Hitler and Mao Tse-tung, a ruthless killer of his own people and others, and a killer of the human spirit. Naegele writes, "When Putin was coming to power, I was told by an old friend on Capitol Hill that he was a "smoother version" of Stalin, and I will never forget those prescient and ominous words." In addition, Naegele correctly defines Putin as a mafia leader and

lists facts of cruelty, which Putin and his Ex-KGB lackeys brought upon Russia and other countries.

90. Then I made decision to tell Olga about my communication with FSB Colonel Polonchuk and the analytical work I did for him. While discussing the events of the past, we came to the conclusion that the FSB persecution began right after I refused to fulfill the FSB order on the Canadian salesman and denied official collaboration with the FSB. Because it was exactly then, in the fall of 2003, that I started having serious problems with my health, which led to the aneurism and inability to work. It was very simple to poison me, as I lived alone in my apartment at that time and it was not difficult for an FSB team to plant poisonous substances when I was out.

91. As we found out from different materials online, the style in which we were poisoned matched completely and exactly the style of killers from Special Services. This conclusion was based on experts' opinion. For example, Russian doctor Baranov V.V. and his wife, scientist-chemist, Baranova T.A accuse Russian special services on their website in widespread secret use of "special substances" and they give detailed information on how special services accomplish poisoning. Quote: "In a democratic society, or a society that has a democratic appearance, the spectrum of traditional methods of pressure on the members of the society is inevitably narrowed, giving way to clandestine means of individual terror known as "the system of outlawed persecution"... In order to create "artificial physical unhealthiness" various means are used, beginning from those that came from the depth of history and ending with modern achievements of genetic engineering... Poisoning by narcotic substances are disguised as epilepsy, stroke, etc., poisonings by metal compounds – as gastroenteritis, peritonitis, etc."

92. The method, which was chosen to kill Olga and I, was unapparent murder, which is a murder nobody can discover to be a murder. It turned out the FSB were disabling my common law wife and I for several years. They were depriving us of our ability to work by regularly poisoning us with small doses of toxic chemical substances. I think they kept poisoning us slowly for several years after I refused to do any more work for the FSB because Polunchuk expected me to come around and change my mind. He wanted us to show that he could control our health, our life, our ability to disseminate our research, and our ability to continue to complete Catalog of Human Population. He expected me to help him. He called me every few months to ask me to help him with a new project. I continued to refuse to help him and mine and Olga's health consequently declined.

93. The analysis of the poisoning issue and chronology of events explained why Olga's health disorders only appeared after she began working with me which was after I declined to use the Catalog of Human Population to fulfill Polunchuk's orders and to officially collaborate with the FSB. Once she and

I were both being poisoned, it is evident that I was being poisoned for much longer than she has been poisoned. We had similar symptoms, but in general my health was significantly worse than her health. She did not have those horrible spasms, which felt as though iron clutches were squeezing my throat and chest almost every night. She also did not have lead and cadmium in her blood. The results of my spirometry established that my bronchial efficiency dropped by 70%. Her respiration was much better than mine.

94. At the beginning this difference confused us; however, soon we realized that prior to us living together, the FSB killers were poisoning only me at my apartment from 2003 to 2009 while I lived alone. Olga's health problems during that time were due to her visiting me at my house but because she kept her own safe apartment, her health was somewhat protected. They started poisoning both of us only after I moved to Olga's apartment. As we found out in special toxicological sources, poisonous substances tend to accumulate in the body and the health condition depends on their quantity.

### Asking for Help and Protection from the Russian Authorities, Medical Professionals, and the Press

95. I believe the FSB or Russian special forces were poisoning us slowly while still giving me a chance to change my mind about working for the FSB. I know that the FSB wanted the Catalog of Human Population for their nefarious activities and I was the key to the Catalog. No me, no Catalog. Polunchuk called every few months and asks me to do work for them. That is how I know they wanted me alive and working. Accordingly, they kept me alive (though barely) and expecting me to choose my health over my own moral principles. I believe that if I had told Polunchuk, during any of the repeated times he called me, that I agreed to work with him again and that and the FSB would have exclusive access to the Catalog of Human Population, that the poisoning would have stopped. Instead, I continued to refuse to help the FSB and the poisoning continued to get worse. Once we started filing reports, going to the press, and asking for help from the police, as explained below, our health only worsened because the poisoning increased. I think Polunchuk and the FSB finally understood we would never help them and as a result, death was the only option. (Fortunately, we fled to the United States before the FSB could execute their final plot against us.)

96. On January 4th 2011, we contacted the police in Moscow as soon as we finally realized what was happening to us. As the owner of the apartment, Olga reported that a crime occurred in connection with the discovery of the

broken lock. The police accepted her statement and took the lock to conduct expert examination. However, on January 13, 2011, prior to getting the results from the expert examination, we received word that our request to initiate criminal proceedings had been denied.

97. Soon thereafter we called in experts from the Moscow Center for Hygiene and Epidemiology. We wanted to find out the condition of our premises and we also hoped that if they found something bad and something out of the ordinary, FSB would be unable to force such a large organization to substitute the results of the examination. Partially, our predictions were correct. Upon conducting three examinations, the experts discovered chemical substances in the quantity, which was hazardous for health and life. They examined the air in the apartment and the air near the carpet, which was initially in the middle of the room and which was later taken out to the balcony; they also examined the air near the bed and in the hallway closet. Excess of the maximum permissible concentration (MPC) in the living premises (room) amounted to: the concentrations of dibutyl phthalate was almost 10 times higher than MPC (carpet examination, which was taken out of the room to the balcony due to the strange smell in the room); the concentration of styrene was 5.5 times higher than MPC (near the bed); the concentration of formaldehyde was 3 times higher than MPC (also near the bed); and the concentration of volatile components of the aromatic mixture was 34 times higher than MPC. Air probes in the closet revealed that the concentration of styrene was 8 times higher than MPC, concentration of naphthalene was 7 times higher than MPC and the concentration of the volatile components of the aromatic mixture was almost 40 times higher.

98. We got this information from the official reports and expert findings as of January 17 and January 26, 2011. Our apartment was officially found inhabitable.

99. However, the examinations into the habitability of our apartment were undermined by the FSB and we believe the final examination was a forgery. The forgery of the last examination (gas chromatography and mass-spectrometry of the carpet), which we requested at the Moscow Center for Hygiene and Epidemiology on January 28, 2011 (carpet sample). We concluded that the forgery was due to, firstly, the fact that we had to wait for a long time for the results. Secondly, when Olga called them again in regards to the delay of the results, the head of the laboratory Andrey Yulievich Poltorackiy told her the lab has experienced big problems because of our request, the lab had to undergo an official inspection (which caused serious problems for their office), and the inspectors demanded withdrawal of the results of the prior examination. Poltorackiy's statements to us led us instantly to conclude the FSB's interference. Only this organization was

capable of forcing such a large and trustworthy governmental establishment as the Moscow Center for Hygiene and Epidemiology to forge documents.

100. While talking to experts from the Moscow Center for Hygiene and Epidemiology, we found out a lot of information, which was not officially documented. <Name>, who was present during all the expert examinations, Olga, and I witnessed the experts' serious confusion regarding the results they obtained. The quantity and the type of substances found in our apartment shocked them much more than us, who were ignorant of the substances' malignancy and unusualness. The experts said that it was the first time they had come across such conditions in a private apartment. The experts did not know how to explain what they had found. Still, they diligently tried to find a reason; for example, they tried to connect such results to the external factors, such that they were probing the air outside of the apartment's window, but they still could not find any explanations despite their varied efforts. In addition, the experts told us that such results could not be connected to furniture, which was more than 15 years old or renovations, which took place in this apartment more than 6 years ago. We were also told that our apartment contained such volatile components of aromatic mixtures 40 times higher than normal, that such was possible through a one-time ejection at a perfumery factory. In response to whether the substances found in our apartment could be considered poisonous and whether they were dangerous for our health, all the experts responded the same thing: given fixated levels of 30 to 40 times higher than norm, all these substances were considered poisonous. The experts recommended escaping our apartment, which they called a "gas chamber," as soon as possible. We instantly remembered the Baranov's article: "In order to create 'artificial physical unhealthiness' various means are used... The spectrum is practically unlimited as all substances if applied in overdoses are toxic for humans." Baranov also stated that these special services were using different poisonous mixtures – multicomponent toxic mixtures." (See Attachment [7].)

101. We also asked the experts how long a person had to inhabit our apartment for the hazardous chemicals to worsen the person's health. They responded that it would take a long time to achieve such results and that application of the poisons required special training. They stated that a non-professional would not be able to achieve such results, but also would be under the risk of poisoning him or herself. They said it would be necessary to regularly refresh poisonous substances to maintain certain concentration. However, the experts refused to tell us as to where such specialists could be trained.

102. We knew the answer to this question ourselves, though: such specialists are trained at FSB. We learned it from the article Special Services against the ordinary people, quote: "As it follows from the open

publications, the most powerful weapons of this system, so called "special means", were and continue to be the weapons developed since the time of Vladimir Lenin in the notorious "Special Office" (Rus: "Spetsialny Kabinet"), which later transformed into top secret toxicological "Laboratory X" of professor Mairanovsky, bacteriological laboratory of academician Muromtsev and so on... Subsequently the weapons were elevated by the modern followers to the qualitatively new level opening a possibility to organize an individual terror on a massive scale." (See "Attachment [7].)

103. For example, we found by some miracle, information about the so-called "Chamber" in an article stating, "Laboratory 12 or Kamera (the Room) was set up in 1921 by the Soviet Secret Service to develop trace-less poisons that would not be evident in an autopsy. The location of this clandestine poison factory is known to few people. As we drove, my contact told me he had worked briefly in the research department and assured me its activities were continuing." (http://www.timesonline.co.uk/tol/news/uk/article1625866.ece) (In Russian: http://www.newsru.com/world/08apr2007/litvi.html) (See: Exhibit ...)

104. We found out that the Special Services of the Russian Federation were using special mixtures of poisonous substances to provoke such symptoms, which regular doctors were unable to understand. These professionals made a "cocktail" of chemical substances in such a way that each "recipe" was tailored for a specific "client" considering his gender, age, health condition, etc. The Baranov's described it as well, writing "During the later Soviet period the Special Services, first of all the KGB, used the data of medical check-ups and physical examinations for active revealing of latent, chronic diseases of a victim with the purpose of their amplification by special means in order to gradually finish off a victim labeling it as death from the natural causes." (See Attachment [7].)

105. We also found out that if some of these ordinary, civilian toxicologists or, for example, experts in forensic medicine managed to uncover secret FSB "cocktails" - the people would either vanish without a trace or they would be found dead. It is mentioned in a lot of literature and we personally encountered the confirmation for it. When we contacted one expert in forensic medicine telling him that we were getting poisoned by Special Services, he not only named an extremely high price for his services, but he also stated that he would never officially document, for any money in the world, what was found in our apartment.

106. Having discovered such a huge amount of poisonous substances in our apartment, we encountered the problem as to how to clear it out of our bodies on our own, without the help of toxicologists who refused to treat us. We found a method, which cleared the blood from any harmful substances – cascade plasma filtration. The procedure purifies the blood by running

the blood through special filters, which retain everything harmful while the beneficial substances and the blood itself are returned to the body of the patient.

107. At the end of January 2011 in the American-Russian outpatient clinic Medsi in Moscow, the transfusiologist Inna Modisovna Mednis heard our complaints, looked through our medical records, and confirmed that cascade plasma filtration was warranted. Olga and I went through the procedure once each. My blood plasma was of such horrific color, that the doctor decided to take a picture of my filter. Inna Modisovna told us she has never seen anything like that before in her life. Due to my plasma filtration results, she gave me a referral to conduct a heavy metal panel. The heavy metal panel showed that I had 40% higher lead content and 20% higher cadmium content than usual. And, these figures were after a complete blood purification procedure! I asked what percentage one procedure of cascade plasma filtration lowers the quantity of heavy metals in blood. The doctor responded that it would be by 20-25%. Thus, prior to the first procedure, I could have the concentration of lead at around 60% higher and the concentration of cadmium at around 40% higher. The doctor confirmed these calculations. She also added that even the quantity that was found after the filtration supported a severe toxic poisoning. In addition, the doctor said that lead and cadmium get deposited not in blood, but in bones and internal organs.

108. On January 28, 2011, the day after we discovered heavy metals in my blood, Olga contacted the police again. Olga filed the second report. We hoped that the police would be able to connect the first statement about lock break with the newly discovered evidence that our apartment contained poisonous substances and that my blood contained lead and cadmium. The first denial in starting the investigation was based on the reason that when Olga submitted the first statement about the break in, there was no indication of burglary. We thought that if the police saw new documents about the poison, then it would be obvious that someone broke into our apartment not for the purpose of taking something out of it, but to plant something – plant the poisonous substances.

109. It turned out that our hopes were futile. On February 8, 2011, we received an official denial of the request to initiate a criminal investigation based on the presence of poisonous substances found in our apartment. The basis for this denial did not tolerate any criticism and it was obviously fabricated. It more resembled idle reasoning and guesses of a police lieutenant, Aleksey Yurevich Nadirov, because they clearly contradicted the conclusions, which experts had made and documented. The lieutenant's conclusions implied the scientific conclusions of the Moscow Center for Hygiene and Epidemiology were incompetent.

110. Sometime after the denial in February 2011, this lieutenant Nadirov, our district police inspector and one other person with captain shoulder straps came to visit us. We were surprised that the district police inspector would come to our home, much less do so accompanied by individuals of higher rank. The police captain seemed very suspicious due to his behavior and the questions he asked. His behavior more resembled that of a FSB agent based on my experience with FSB agents. The incident strengthened our opinion that the FSB or similar organization was working against us.

111. During the period of December 2010 through the end of March 2011, Olga and I felt like handcuffed prisoners. Beginning December 2010 we stopped going outside together. We would go outside alone only when it was necessary (buy groceries, visit doctors, etc.). We were doing it in order to prevent our killers from breaking into our apartment.

112. In addition, I could not go outside because of my serious problems breathing while walking. Olga was buying groceries and medicine. Once she would come back, she had to completely undress right at the entrance and take a shower right away; she would also wash all the clothes that she was wearing to go outside. Due to such special nature of the events, she had to wear only light windbreakers even when it was freezing outside because she could not wash a fur coat, sheepskin coat, or feather down-padded coat.

113. Olga and a person who would accompany her (she stopped leaving the apartment without a companion) were forced to stop using cell phones. We noticed that our cell phones were not only tapped, but were also used as special microphones, through which our persecutors were able to follow everything that was happening in our apartment and follow the destinations of owners of these phones. Our connection to the outside world was completely interrupted.

114. After some time, Olga practically stopped going outside because we were afraid of more cardinal actions on the part of our murderers especially after contacting official organizations and seeing their reaction to our requests for help. Elena Skorbatyuk (Olga's daughter) and our acquaintances <name> and her daughter <name> brought us groceries and medicine.

115. In addition, Olga and I were forced to stop communicating with our parents, since we were afraid that someone would persecute them as well. Our communication circle was very narrow: Olga's daughter, two acquaintances who were helping us during these difficult times, who I mentioned above; the therapist Klochkova, O.L, who was trying to treat us somehow, and our lawyer <name>. Our lawyer was helping us with solving issues with the police and other governmental agencies, which we were forced to contact. Based on our observation, a person or persons were planting poisons on the people in our circle since they became sick as well. For example, <name>'s spirometry detected bronchial obstruction,

although her bronchi were normal in the past, she did not smoke (please refer to <name>'s testimonial evidence for more details). When murderers from FSB were forced to stop using their previous methods of poisoning us because one of us was always at the apartment and they could no longer sneak in while we were out, they started poisoning everybody who was entering and leaving our apartment in order to get the poisons still into our apartment. We also received certain "packages" brought our guests as "mailmen." However, due to the fact that Olga and I accumulated much more poisonous substances in our bodies than our guests by that time (and the "cocktails" were created for us and not for them), our health worsened to a much greater extent than those others in our circle.

116. We stopped using phone connections and we contacted people through multiple electronic mailboxes. Our acquaintances experienced strange incidents and malfunctions of their mobile and Internet connections. For example, one day when Olga woke up, she saw a missed call from <name>. She called <name> back but she told Olga that she did not call her. They were both confused. Later they resolved it. <name> told us, that once she hung up after talking to Olga, she reviewed all her outgoing calls. She discovered not only Olga's number, which she has never dialed, but she also saw as right in front of her eyes this number was getting erased from her phone. Additionally, another time we unplugged the Internet connection cord from our computer; however the computer was still connected and was able to open up Internet pages. I experienced multiple examples like the ones described above.

117. In February 2011, apparently after our murderers made certain that we not only discovered their plan, but we were also trying to report what was happening to us – we noticed a light on at the attic of the house across. (We have a picture). At the same time we noticed that our enemies could get the information not only through the conversations on the cell phones but also through conversations that took place at home. It forced us to think whether "internal sound bugs" were installed in our apartment. We felt that we could no longer speak freely in the apartment. We kept a notebook and a pencil on the kitchen table and we started communicating with each other and our few acquaintances exclusively in writing.

118. Later after this, more things happened which supported our fears that we were being poisoned and watched. We started hearing strange noises that were coming from the apartment upstairs where nobody lived for a long time. We also noticed that when we were sleeping with the balcony door open, we would always wake up really beat and I would have even stronger and more frequent suffocation fits. We remembered the information from the Baranov's website: "If there is no possibility to intrude into the dwelling, poisoning substances are usually delivered as vapor or aerosol via the ventilation system of the building, or by a special drill that

can run through a residence ceiling or a wall, or by other methods." (See Attachment [7].) Olga tried to call the neighbor above, but he would not pick up his phone. Then she contacted the property management who informed Olga that according to their information this apartment was currently empty. We also discovered new strange similar stains above our main entrance door and on the kitchen ceiling. All our houseplants turned yellow, dried out and died (we have pictures). All of this led us to conclude that we had to leave our apartment as soon as possible.

## The Final Months in Russia

119. Late on the night of February 11, 2011, without any word, with our phones turned off, and taking only minimal necessities with us, Olga and I left our apartment for good. We moved to the apartment of <name>, who agreed to give us shelter at: ...

120. This arrangement significantly helped us to survive. Upon entering <name>'s apartment, we instantly noticed that the atmosphere there was quite different from what we were used to. And we immediately realized the reason: the air in <name>'s apartment was fresh. It did not contain unpleasant or heavy smells like those in our apartment. We found ourselves thinking that, after a few months of confinement, we practically had forgotten the taste of normal air.

121. Time passed, and being that it is inappropriate to live in somebody else's apartment for a long time and we could not go back anymore to our apartment, we had no place to live. We had to do something. So we tried to get attention of law enforcement agencies yet again and to obtain their protection. In the middle of February of 2011, Olga filed a third statement with the police. Olga filed the statements because she owned the apartment.

122. We also contacted journalist Alexander Lebedev (http://www.alebedev.org/), who is the owner of Novaya Gazeta (New Newspaper) (http://en.novayagazeta.ru/). We provided him with materials about our medical problems, the police reports and responses, the letters to the President and Prime Minister, and about my relationship with Colonel Polunchuk of the FSB. I was not afraid that Mr. Lebedev would alert the FSB about my claims because I myself was already telling the FSB I was aware of their actions and I thought that if my story made the press, then the FSB would back off. I thought publishing our story would protect us. Mr. Lebedev responded that he received the materials and they were interesting to him so he personally gave them to his editors. The editors contacted us by phone and said that our information was interesting, but they needed some clarifications before publishing our story and that they

would call us back. But then we were forced to turn our phones off again and our connection to the journalists was interrupted. Since we could not use or trust our phones, we decided that it was useless to contact other magazines or newspapers.

123. On March 3, 2011, without any response from the police, we sent a letter to President A.D. Medvedev and Prime-Minister V.V. Putin.

124. In the middle of March 2011 we received a response from the presidential reception that they directed this case to police. It was the dead end. In regards to Putin's reception, despite the law, which requires this governmental agency to respond to the appeals of all citizens, we did not receive any response to our appeal.

125. I would like to reiterate that all our statements to official agencies were sent with the copies of the expert medical examinations. Thus, we presented the proof that Olga and I were being poisoned to death. None of the governmental agencies responded. None of them came to our aid. None of them tried to protect us. None of these myrmidons of the law, these blind agencies cogs – i.e. from the police from the Novo-Peredelkino District, public prosecutor's office, MVD, Moscow Center for Hygiene and Epidemiology, Presidential reception and Prime Minister reception – were going to interfere with the activities of the FSB. The abovementioned agencies deliberately left us, who were sick and absolutely helpless, alone against the FSB who were trained professionals attempting to kill us slowly in a professional and purposeful manner. This was all done despite the existence of the European Convention on Human Rights, which includes such rights as the "right to life," "right to security of person," "right to security of residence," and "right to security of personal privacy." Despite the proof that our constitutional rights were violated, none of the governmental agencies responded to our multiple statements and none of them protected us.

126. In March 2011, we took one last step. We sent a letter to the FSB of the Russian Federation. However, we did not wait for their response (and as it turned out later we did the right thing, because the FSB supposedly conducted the verification in a very short period of time and based on this verification denied further investigation). Due to all the actions that we took, our lives were in even greater danger than before. Once we realized the mortal danger has increased, we had nothing else to do but to leave our Russia forever. We exhausted all the chances of survival in this country; the country, where governmental agencies, which were called for protecting its citizens by law, were killing them with impunity.

127. We had to act with no delays. Despite our bad health conditions – I could barely breathe and Olga was not in the best shape either – we had nothing else to do but to escape, leaving everything behind. At that time we

had only one visa in our passports – American visa, which was still open from the last visit.

## Fleeing Russia for the United States

128. The night between March 30th and March 31st of 2011 Olga called the taxi company from the new phone, which she specifically bought for this purpose, using somebody else's name and address and not stating to the operator as to where we were going. (We knew that these companies were monitored as well and if Olga used her real name and address, FSB would find out about it immediately.) Olga met the taxi at the indicated place and then they drove to the place, where I was waiting for them with all our things. (This time we had to pack only for carry on, we packed our things considering the fact that it would be dangerous to check in our luggage; we knew that FSB agents watched every airport and they could have access to the luggage of any passenger and might poison our luggage.) Once we left our place, we told the driver that we had to go the Domodedovo airport as opposed to Kiev Station as Olga has told to the operator. Thus, we were able to get to the airport without any obstacles.

129. We arrived there 2 hours prior to departure (we knew all the departure times in advance), we purchased two tickets from Singapore airlines (since we knew Aeroflot planes always had former KGB agents on board) to Houston in the United States of America and left Russia for what must be the last time.

130. However, we chose not to stay long in Houston because the Moscow airport records showed us to be in Houson. That is why, despite the fact that we felt really bad, we took another flight to San Diego. The choice of the location was made partially because of the climate, which was recommended by our doctors and partially because our acquaintances lived there and without them our stay in the United States would be very difficult since we spoke only very little English.

131. Nobody knew about our departure: parents, children, people, in whose apartment we lived for the last month and a half, none of them knew. We did not have a chance to say goodbye to our relatives. Even now our parents do not know where we are and what is happening to us. And we have not known, for several months now, if they are ok, if they are healthy and alive. However, our flee from Russia was a desperate measure that allowed us to leave Russia successfully and come to the United States. It was equally dangerous for them and us to communicate with each other: all phones, electronic mailboxes, and physical mail of our relatives and acquaintances were still monitored by FSB.

132. As a result of Olga's and my confidentiality, the efficiency of our actions, and our swiftness, which the Special Services of the Russian

Federation did not expect from two seriously ill people, we managed to escape from Russia.

## Conclusion

133. I believe that here, in the United States, Olga and I have a chance at survival. Since arriving in the United States, I have felt a sense of security and safety that I had not felt in a very long time. I no longer have to fear being attacked or poisoned. We have a chance at living a normal life where nobody forces entry into our house and nobody plants any poison. We miss our families and our homeland, but we know that if we return to our homeland, I am certain Olga and I will be killed as soon as we return. We can never go back. The FSB knows that we will never help them. They know that we fled from them and that we escaped their poisonous net and murderous plot against our lives. They know that we are telling the truth about what they did to us and what they tried to do to us. Going back to Russia as enemies of the FSB, who operate with total impunity within Russia, would be a death sentence for us.

134. Based on all that has transpired, I respectfully request that the Asylum Office grant me asylum so that I may continue to live safely in the United States.

Thank you for your attention.

Respectfully,

Andrey Nikolaevich Davydov
Originally drafted July 4, 2011.
Revised and signed February 21, 2012

## Referenced Materials/Attachments ... :

[1] His name is Alexandr Gritsak (http://vk.com/id14576155). He is one of the people, whom we suspect were involved in attacks made on our website and is part of the group led by Colonel A. D. Polonchuk. This group of FSB

employees most likely also includes the following people: Alexey Sobolev (http://vk.com/deep_stagnum, http://www.facebook.com/jazz.claimber), Anton Sobolev (http://vk.com/id11648088), Olga Apenko (married name Soboleva - http://vk.com/olga_soboly, http://www.facebook.com/olga.apollin, http://www.facebook.com/olga.apenko), Igor Shushlyapin (http://vk.com/id5387685, http://www.facebook.com/profile.php?id=100005738349182), Rasul Rizvanov (http://vk.com/id16071198, http://www.facebook.com/rasik.dakas), Natalia Hramtsova (http://vk.com/nhramtsova, http://www.facebook.com/natalia.hramtsova), Mikhail Zotin (http://vk.com/id171516, http://www.facebook.com/mihail.zotin.3), Nadezhda Abramova (http://www.facebook.com/nadezhda.abramova).

[2] According to "Global Financial Integrity" (GFI), around $427 billions of dollars were transferred from Russia from 2000 to 2008. http://www.gazeta.ru/financial/2011/04/01/3572005.shtml). V.V. Putin couldn't go past the fact that, even according to official sources, large monitory amounts did not accumulate in his pocket. The official version of Putin's estate is in order: he supposedly lives on his salary; he has governmental provisions and apartment. The official information about the cost of the Presidential election champagne is as modest as official Putin's financial condition; however, the real funds spent on his election champagne are, in total, not less than official funds spent on election champagnes by presidents of other countries (United States, France, Italy and so on). Although these funds are used illegally in Russia, and Putin, occupying the presidential post, could not or didn't want to change this specificity. Moreover, as to the billions of dollars, which were transferred illegally, Putin decided to use it for his personal enrichment, using the potential of his dear organization FSB. The act of confiscating financial means from Russian citizens took many forms: if someone couldn't understand what Putin wanted, he would quickly lose money and life at the same time; someone, who would resist for a short period of time, would lose health and money, but would save the life; and someone who would immediately understand and agree to serve Putin would save health, life, business and a portion of money. An example to that would be well-known Roman Abramovich, who is included in the list of the richest people of the world in the magazine "Forbs." Many people know about Abramovich's famous purchase of the English soccer team "Chelsea" in 2003 and purchase of famous players in the world, which cost him around 1 billion of American dollars. However, not everybody knows that when Putin was Russian President, Abramovich was the governor of Chukchi Peninsula (he was elected as the governor of Chukchi Peninsula on December 24th 2000). As the governor of the Chukchi Peninsula, he invested much more

of his personal capital into the development of this district than in "Chelsea." During his 7 year service as the governor, Abramovich invested around $2.5 billion in Chukotka, based on the most modest calculations. While occupying the post of the governor, Abramovich asked for resignation multiple times, however President Putin didn't grant it to him. But he "granted" the permission to invest around 3 billion dollars of Abramovich's personal capital in Chukotka during his two terms as a governor. I never heard of the precedent when governors of other countries, for example in the United States, were forced to invest personal capital in the districts under their control and without any chance of getting this money back. Abramovich is an example of the Russian businessman, who didn't want to get killed and rubbed by President Putin and his gang from FSB; he is one of those who willingly gave Putin a portion of his money.

[3] At that time I was offered to conduct analytical research of options of physical elimination of one Canadian businessman. I wasn't offered the role of a hired killer, but, in essence, if I would have agreed to it, I would be indirectly involved in the murder. I decided that there was a talk about physical elimination (murder) because of some details of the conversation about this research, which I was offered to do. For example, they were interested in the type of medical examination of the corps of this businessman; I had a specific task – the diagnosis must have indicated natural cause of death, not violent death in any case.

[4] You can find more information about our research and about the Catalog of Human Population on our website at http://www.catalogofhumanpopulation.org [Note: the website URL is now http://www.humanpopulationacademy.org]

[5] Links to the materials found online:

1. Timothy D. Naegele, Naegeleblog, "Russia's Putin is a Killer" - http://naegeleblog.wordpress.com/2010/02/09/russias-putin-is-a-killer/

2. "Russia's Killing Ways" Washington Post - http://www.washingtonpost.com/wp-dyn/content/article/2006/12/13/AR2006121301909.html

3. The New York Sun, "Russian's killing methods" - http://www.nysun.com/opinion/russias-killing-methods/44681/

4. The information about the fact that Russian FSB is the organizer of terrorist acts, kidnapping and murders; about the book "FSB is blowing up Russia" A. Litvinenko published in London "Blowing Up Russia: The Secret Plot to Bring Back KGB Terror" - http://www.guardian.co.uk/theobserver/2007/jan/21/politics

5. "Power and absolute corruption" - http://entertainment.timesonline.co.uk/tol/arts_and_entertainme nt/books/article1291906.ece.

6. The article about special services using poisoning to accomplish contract killings (there is English version there as well) http://www.novayagazeta.ru/data/2006/91/00.html

7. The article about how Kremlin "eliminates" those who fall out of its favor http://news.liga.net/smi/NP060236.html

8. "Special Services against the Ordinary People". Detailed information about the ways of how Russian special services use poisonous substances to kill peaceful Russian citizens, with big bibliography about poisonings. http://www.baranovfamily.org/, http://www.baranovfamily.org/findings_eng.html The story of the Baranov's poisoning, which became the precedent to start the process in the Los Angeles court - http://www.baranovfamily.org/strasbourgCase_eng.html. The list of people who were poisoned for Russian special services http://www.baranovfamily.org/announcements_eng.html

9. Different examples of poisoning:

The poisoning of Kalashnikov, former FSB officer and his wife - http://www.youtube.com/watch?v=P54Dj3XAqFM&NR=1

Poisoning of Russian Journalist Yury Shchekochikhin http://www.eng.yabloko.ru/Publ/2004/PAPERS/07/040702_mt.h tml

Poisoning of Litvinenko. Newspaper "The Independent" – "Litvinenko's death: the toxic legacy" (In English) http://www.independent.co.uk/news/uk/crime/litvinenko s-death-the-toxic-legacy-760114.html.

The article from "Washington Post" "Radioactive Poison Killed Ex-Spy" - http://www.washingtonpost.com/wp-dyn/content/article/2006/11/24/AR2006112400410.html

The article "Poisoning of Alexander Litvinenko", which specifically states that his murder was accomplished by Russian special services agents http://tribuna.com.ua/articles/conflicts/103961.htm

Article from Wikipedeia "Poisoning of Alexandr Litvinenko" (in English) http://en.wikipedia.org/wiki/Poisoning_of_Alexander_Litvinenko

Video from Youtube, which is composed of several parts, called "In memory of Litvinenko, who was murdered," where Litvinenko directly says that FSB is the gang, which is hired for contract murder http://www.youtube.com/watch?v=BQr47Kd3PQ8 (in Russian). In

English:
http://www.youtube.com/watch?v=tj9YzwPAA_M&feature=related
, http://www.youtube.com/watch?v=BQr47Kd3PQ8, Litvinenko
talks about FSB crimes.
http://www.youtube.com/watch?v=WmbgGsvuUZ8&feature=relate
d.

10. Articles, which directly state as to who is dealing with poisoning
and how it is accomplished -
http://www.newsru.com/world/08apr2007/litvi.html (in Russian),
"The Laboratory 12 poison plot" (in English),
http://www.timesonline.co.uk/tol/news/uk/article1625866.ece (in
English).

11. Articles, which state that Russian special services poison not only
in Russia and not only Russians, but everybody who is out of their
favor. For example, president of the European Court
http://www.guardian.co.uk/world/2007/feb/01/russia.topstories3;
about Karina Moskalenko "Russian suspects poisoning"-
http://articles.latimes.com/2008/oct/16/world/fg-poison16

12. Case of scientists who got killed (Pasechnik)
http://www.stevequayle.com/index.php?s=145 (English),
http://emigration.russie.ru/news/3/7223_1.html (Pasechnik story
in Russian).

13. The article about how FSB is poisoning those who escaped
abroad - http://www.city-n.ru/view/166179.html

14. In short, about the situation in Russia. About how Russian
scientists are being killed because the have secret knowledge (In
Russian:
http://infosmi.com/news/read/Russkih_uchenyh_ubivajut_iz_za_
sekretnyh_dannyh_Uzhe_5_zhertv.html); about how many people
are disappearing in Russia without any trace (In Russian, article
translated from "Observe" -
http://www.inosmi.ru/untitled/20030105/168280.html); about
Russia being the leader on the slave-trading market (http://forum-
msk.org/material/society/2517669.html).

15. About FSB, in English
http://911review.org/Wiki/FSBThreatWithinRussia.shtml

[6] V.V. Putin officially joined KGB when he was 23 years old, he
made his career there, he became the chief of this agency at the end
of 90-s, and from there he became the Russian President. That is
why, when he became the President, he didn't rely on MVD or public
prosecutor's office. After he got to know KGB power and after being
raised by this structure, he, having power of the President of the

country, reoriented all the actions of this agency in his personal interests. All the more so, since not MVD or any other Russian organization but former KGB, present FSB, act equally freely not only inside of Russia but also abroad, including the United States.

[7] Baranovs' article "Special Services against the ordinary people" http://www.baranovfamily.org/index.html

[8] About FSB toxicological laboratory http://www.glavred.info/archive/2006/12/01/140308-0.html, http://www.dopinfo.ru/useful/cognitive01/17.php (in Russian)."

# CHAPTER 3

# STORY FROM POLITICAL CASE OF OLGA SKORBATYUK—ANDREY DAVYDOV'S COLLEAGUE IN SCIENTIFIC RESEARCH

### "Declaration

I, the undersigned, declare the following to be true and correct to the best of my recollection under penalty of perjury:

## Introduction

1. I am a forty-four year old citizen and native of the Russia Federation. My complete name is Olga Vladimirovna Skorbatyuk.   ... I was born in Moscow. I was raised in Moscow by my parents <name> and <name>. I have no siblings. My parents still live in Moscow. My daughter lives in Moscow. Unfortunately, I have little or no contact with my parents and daughter because I fear that interacting with them will cause them to be targeted by the same group trying to kill me.

2. I came to the United States in 2009 and 2010, both times on a B-2 visa. I did not apply for asylum on either of those trips because at the time I was not completely sure that forces were trying to kill my partner Andrey Nikolaevich Davydov ("Andrey") and I on account of our scientific research, as explained below, and the opposition research he provided to the Russian FSB, as explained below. I then came again to the United States on March 31, 2011 in B-2 status with permission to remain in the United States until September 30, 2011. I came to the United States at that time with my partner, Andrey Nikolaevich Davydov ("Andrey"), so both of us could apply for political asylum together.

3. We have since met with various attorneys regarding our fear of life in the Russian Federation and began to prepare our applications, declarations, and supporting documents, in order to file the documents within one year of our entry to the United States. This declaration is written in support of my application for asylum. As a trained scientist, I have tried to be as detailed as possible, but I can further explain any of the points of this declaration in greater detail if asked to do so.

## Formal Education and Work Experience

4. I received my formal education in Moscow and attended excellent schools. I received high marks in school and graduated with honors. Growing up, I looked repeatedly for ways to help me with self-realization and self-development. I searched for the answer to the questions of 'who I was,' 'what was my life's purpose,' and 'in what way could I transform into an individual with new qualities?' I studied and practiced multiple psychological, philosophical and religious concepts: psychoanalysis, Zen Buddhism, Taoism, yoga, Christianity and some other concepts, which relate to the human psyche, but never managed to answer my life's questions. I remained disappointed on my path: I could not find anything to help me in getting answers to my questions nor a specific recipe for solving my problems. I decided that I needed an in-depth study in order to determine what the human soul was and its structure and I applied and got admitted to the Moscow Institute of Psychology and Pedagogy to get a degree in Practical Psychology. I began my coursework in September 2000 and graduated in July 2007.

5. My education in psychology did not answer my life's questions. In my fourth year at the Institute, I became very worried because of the Institute's ability to provide the education I really sought. The Institute did not help me to learn who I was, why I was born, or about other people and how to communicate with them. I worried that I would be unable to help my future clients to solve their psychological problems even after graduating from the Institute and becoming a professional psychologist. In addition to not figuring out my life's questions, The Institute did not teach a working method to understand future clients and solve their problems either. Other students at the Institute shared my worries.

6. Fortunately, in 2003 my introduction to one man would change the course of my life, answer my questions, and show me the method by which I could understand and help future clients. But his work that I embraced and the person that he was would also come to put my life at risk. That man is Andrey Nikolaevich Davydov (Andrey). In November 2003, an acquaintance of mine in Moscow, <name>, introduced me to Andrey who was conducting very interesting work at that time. Andrey had already received national recognition as the discoverer and primary researcher of the Catalog of Human Population. He was in fact decoding the ancient manuscript Shan Hai Jing (also referred to as Classic of the Mountains and Seas). As a trained psychologist, I became very interested in the topic of his research – the Catalog of Human Population. In short, the Catalog of Human Population thoroughly describes the entire human subconscious motivational sphere in great detail. <name> was testing the Catalog of Human Population on herself and her acquaintances and it turned out to be accurate. I was really intrigued. Every psychologist is in search of a unique

method – a tool for comprehending somebody else's' soul and the overall understanding of what the soul (psyche) of the person is and what kind of structure it has. Through my experience, I had previously concluded a psychologist had to know exactly who was in front of him, who the patient really was, what the patient might be hiding behind his/her numerous masks, and what his/her true motivations are, in order to be able to help. Thun, I met Andrey Nikolaevich and became acquainted with the Catalog of Human Population, which he was decoding in his "Totems" laboratory.

7. In December of 2003, in order to test Andrey's theory, my psychologist colleagues and I ordered some materials. The results exceeded our expectations: absolutely all descriptions of people, whom Andrey never met, turned out to be 100% accurate. We, professional psychologists, were totally amazed and began considering the possibilities of analyzing the structure of the human psyche through this tool developed by Andrey. Our results qualified his many years (beginning in 1975) of research into the ancient Chinese text Shan Hai Jing and proved the ancient book to be a valuable and unique psychological Catalog of the psyches of the entire human population. My colleagues and I came to the same conclusion: the descriptions of personalities, derived from Andrey's methodology gave a complete understanding as to who that person was, his/her individual characteristics, his/her internal motives, his/her life algorithms, his/her desires, his/her aspirations, his/her secret passions and how he/she accomplished all of it in his/her real life. Andrey's thesis that all people are bio-machines operating within human programs was undisputed by factual proof capable of being replicated by other scientists. I was so impressed by what I saw that at the beginning of 2004, I contacted Andrey asking him if I could participate in his research.

8. I remember that during one of our initial conversations, Andrey mentioned that an acquaintance of his, a representative of what I thought to be Russian Special Forces and ultimately proved to be Russian Federal Security Services ("FSB"), the legacy KGB, (he avoided mentioning first and last names and other details in conversations with me for quite a while) was very interested in the Catalog and that he was offering financial support for this research. Andrey did not tell me out of pride or arrogance, but I knew that Andrey appreciated that the Russian Special Forces had a trust and interest in his work. Andrey told me he declined monetary assistance from the FSB to set up the laboratory because he did not want to support or be forced to assist in some of their illegal and illicit activities. Everyone in Russia knows that the FSB operates outside of the law and with impunity. The FSB can do whatever it wants, but chooses to act in secrecy nearly all of the time. When he originally told me about his involvement with the FSB, I gave the relationship little importance. I was more interested in the Shan Hai Jing-derived Catalog and the possibilities it provided. Particularly

because Andrey told me that his communication with this acquaintance ended in approximately 2000. I also remember that *<name>*, who introduced me to Andrey, hinted Andrey was communicating with Special Forces; however, the prospect of working with the Catalog of Human Population  and the possibility of unrestricted access to the information it could reveal overshadowed any fear of danger that I felt regarding Andrey's association with the FSB.

9. I began to directly participate in the creation of Catalog of Human Population decryptions using Shan Hai Jing. Once I began studying the Catalog of Human Population, I quickly advanced in the understanding of the human psyche and how it worked.  Thus, even as a mere senior at the Institute I began writing scientific articles with Andrey. Together, we created several articles related to Catalog of Human Population including but not limited to:

- From Carl Gustav Jung's Archetypes of the Collective Unconscious to Individual Archetypical Patterns.
- Archetype Semantics: How it Relates to the Notion of Image.
- How Archetypical Are Images?
- Could Archetypal Images Have Chimeric Depiction?
- Society as Manipulating and Manipulated Community.

The articles related to Catalog of Human Population are also included along with my declaration along with their English summary translations.  All of our articles are copyrighted under the Russian Community of Author's Rights. We paid to have the articles to be copyrighted. We did not profit from the articles. The articles were written in preparation for the book. The only magazine that paid for any of Andrey's articles was Oracle. Andrey and I have planned to include our articles related to Catalog of Human Population as chapters in the upcoming book Manual of Non-traditional Psychoanalysis.  Our upcoming book which has not been finished due to the events explained below, will serve to inform the worldwide scientific circles about the breakthrough that is the Catalog of Human Population and the compilation of our articles will serve as the factual foundation for the beginning of yet another scientific direction in psychology based on the decryption of Shan Hai Jing.  I presented the first article I wrote (as mentioned above) to my teachers at the Institute.  I received only positive feedback and compliments.  My teachers were astonished with the depth of the subject and the knowledge I had about it.  They gave me a high grade for my work, which was to describe Andrey's research product from the scientific, psychological point of view.  Their initial praise inspired me to continue writing about our scientific research and to complete the other articles listed above.

10. In approximately February-March of 2004, Andrey and I started a personal relationship. I was so interested in Andrey, both him and his work, that I pursued him. He was separated with two children at the time. I was also not married. I was divorced when Andrey and I began dating. Our work and our relationship made us inseparable. We did not start living together until July 2009 when Andrey moved in with me.

11. In 2005 while I was still a student at the Institute, Andrey and I made the decision to write and publish the series of books, in which we presented the possibilities of our technology. The books were unlike the articles in that they were written to be read by the non-scientific community in easby o understand language. The books were written using strict scientific language just like our previous articles, bu we also wanted content about the Catalog of Human Population to be generally accessible so that anybody could read about Catalog. We created four books about: (i) people born on April 5th leap years and April 6th common years; (ii) people born on March 22nd leap years and March 23rd common years; (iii) people born on December 6th leap years and December 7th common years; and (iv) people born October 12th leap years and October 13th common years. These books were written using popular scientific language and they were called Manipulative Games for Women because we thought that the title would get the attention of women and increase sales and allow us to more widely disseminate the information. The books were published by a Moscow publisher. We spent about $10,000 to publish 16,000 copies (4,000 of each book) and each book was sold for $2 to $5 dollars. We paid for the publishing and production. Unfortunately, half of the copies were stolen. Many of the books sold, but we ultimately lost money on the book sales because of the theft as well as for the reasons described below.

12. I was also interested in writing my candidate's and doctoral dissertations on the topic of the Catalog of Human Population as my postgraduate study. However, all the events, explained below, prevented me from doing so. Despite my complex understanding of the Catalog of Human Population, my belief in its positive practical application, and extensive writing and research on the topic, I still completed all the requisite courses of studies in general psychology taught by the Institute, passed all the exams, and wrote a thesis on the psychology of management in order to graduate, which I did in 2007.

13. In terms of information and practice, I never came back to the Institute's version of psychology nor used the methods of traditional psychology as a psychologist. Instead I was using Andrey's methodology, the Catalog of Human Population, exclusively. From 2004, when I began seeing clients, until 2011 when I came to the United States, I applied the mechanics of Catalog of Human Population to my clients without difficulties and with success. Through the Catalog of Human Population, I

always knew who I was dealing with and how to communicate with him/her; I had a clear understanding of my clients' true motivations, desires and aspirations; and how I could help them. During my practice as a psychologist, I did not have a single client who left disappointed or unsatisfied to my knowledge. Thanks to the Catalog of Human Population I was never ashamed for myself or for my work, because my work was not based on my subjective opinions about one or another person and his or her situations, but instead was based on the information from the Catalog of Human Population as derived from Shan Hai Jing (Classic of the Mountains and Seas). I believe that is why my clients paid significant amounts, even in a most terrible economy, for information from the Catalog of Human Population about themselves and their relatives. Accordingly, through my knowledge and experience in how to apply the unique and universal Catalog of Human Population as a tool, I was able to help my clients.

## Involvement with the FSB and Consequent Persecution

14. Over the course of our relationship, Andrey told me more about his involvement with the Special Forces or FSB. He told me that it all began in June or July 2000 when Andrey was approached by FSB (Russian Federal Security Services, former KGB) colonel Andrey Dmitrievich Polonchuk. Colonel Polunchuk has heard about Andrey's work on the Catalog of Human Population through the article published in Fortitude and contacted him by phone at his apartment. As part of the FSB, it was easy for the Colonel to get his private number. The Colonel asked Andrey to provide him with a personality analysis of Putin using Andrey's unique method which he developed through his work on the Catalog of Human Population. Putin came to power in May 2000 and Polonchuk was interested in knowing what the possibilities were of Putin remaining in power for a long period of time, what kind of personal capital the new President had, how he obtained it, how he used his financial resources, and where he kept it. Through using the Catalog of Human Population to analyze behavior patterns of people using a special estimation methodology developed by Andrey; the analysis can foretell activities, such as vicious or illegal activities. Andrey provided this type of personality analysis about Putin to FSB agent Polonchuk at the agent's request. Colonel Polunchuk paid Andrey for his work. Although Andrey did not know whether Polunchuk wanted Putin in power or not, he knew that Polunchuk wanted to be on the side of power so if Putin was going to remain in power, then Polunchuk would support him.

15. Andrey's analysis about Putin based on the Catalog of Human Population deduced that Putin was the theoretical and practical mastermind behind terrorist acts in his country and abroad. The analysis

also provided insight regarding the source of the financial assets that Putin possessed: from where he obtained them, how he was able to accumulate them, and how he used them. The analysis deduced Putin's financial fortune was based on the use of the FSB as an instrument to coerce funds from some Russian citizens and through illegally transferring large amounts of money abroad from and within the Russian Federation. The analysis provided additional information that citizens who were trying to resist Putin's robbery were eliminated with impunity and their money was transferred to Putin's personal accounts abroad.

16. Andrey continued to do several more analysis projects for Colonel Polunchuk during the next four years. The Colonel always paid cash when the work performed. He paid between ... per project. The most expensive work regarded high profile cases about terrorists. The high profile work, such as the work regarding terrorists, was delivered to Andrey's or the Colonel's apartment. The low-profile projects were delivered during meetings at cafes. He always picked up the work himself at Andrey's apartment.

17. After four years of passing analytical information, first without my assistance and later based on our collaborative work, provided to colonel Polonchuk, Andrey refused to provide any further analytical information to the colonel because he felt that the information requested, if provided, would result in criminal acts and even murder. Polonchuk and his FSB colleagues were planning on using the Catalog of Human Population as a powerful tool to engage in negative activities such as theft, all types of violence, and murder of those people who opposed Putin and for accomplishing other criminal activities. And subsequently, Andrey refused to sign an official collaboration agreement with the FSB. So after providing information to Colonel Polunchuk from 2000 until 2004, Andrey stopped cooperating.

18. Andrey did not know at that time that his refusal to continue to provide information and analysis derived based on the Catalog of Human Population to the FSB was tantamount to a death sentence for him and me. His knowledge of the FSB and refusal to enable the criminal acts of the FSB was compromising to FSB generals and high-level Russian executives. Additionally, a second reason why the FSB colonel wanted us eliminated was because the colonel ordered information from Andrey about Putin. Polunchuk wanted Andrey and I out of the picture because he never wanted Putin to find out that Polunchuk ordered an analysis of Putin and that Polunchuk had ever doubted Polunchuk. The colonel wanted us out of the picture because he feared that through Andrey or I, Putin would discover the colonel's group's attitudes, plans, and past actions. Furthermore, the colonel hinted to Andrey that the FSB strongly objected to the general public finding out about the existence of this ancient

source of knowledge which helped analyze the nature and structure of the human psyche, in other words the Catalog of Human Population, because they felt they could lose their power. Since Andrey was unwilling to further enable the FSB's criminal activities through his providing of analysis, and due to the fact that Polonchuk realized during the time of working with Andrey that Polunchuk's own analysts were not capable of obtaining the information through the Catalog of Human Population without Andrey's help, Polonchuk decided to act based on the principle: "If not ours, then nobody's." Therefore, the FSB decided to eliminate Andrey and I.

## Life and the Catalog of Human Population After Refusing the FSB

19. After discontinuing any relationship with Colonel Polunchuk and the FSB, Andrey's and my health both rapidly declined.

20. From mid-2004 through 2005, Andrey's severe health complications forced us to stop creating the complete version of the Catalog of Human Population. When we stopped working on the Catalog of Human Population only 50 of the 293 human programs described in Shan Hai Jing (Classic of the Mountains and Seas) were decoded. However, as soon as he started feeling better, he offered to write a series of scientific articles not to further waste any time.

21. In Fall 2005, we created the website "The Catalog of Human Population," where any guest can find out about this discovery and also could have the possibility to test for themselves the possibilities of the technology we extrapolated from Shan Hai Jing (Classic of the Mountains and Seas). Although we had not decrypted many of the human programs when we put up the website we felt there were enough decrypted programs from our point of view to give an idea to people as to what we offered. The test was simple and did not require any special means or special education. After reviewing a short video, any interested person can compare the descriptions offered in order to verify the accuracy of our understanding of the Catalog of Human Population based on the Shan Hai Jing (Classic of the Mountains and Seas).

22. Also, at the beginning of fall 2005, I offered this information to the media. Almost instantly, in October of 2005, I was invited to appear on a TV show. I appeared on the Moscow TV channel TDK. Andrey thought it was better that I appear on the television and he research. Andrey had previously taped two different television shows on Russia's premier channel with well-respected directors but the shows were never aired so Andrey did not want to spend any more time on the television shows. I appeared in a series of TV shows dedicated to our scientific work. The live shows were

60-minute episodes and comprised of me talking about the theory of Catalog of Human Population while giving examples of descriptions of human programs. My shows were a success. The shows captured high ratings among viewers; based on what the editor of the shows later told me as well as the hearty response from viewers. There were a lot of calls during the live broadcast. People, who were rather surprised with and puzzled by the accuracy of the descriptions. Nobody called to say the information was wrong or incomplete; on the contrary callers confirmed the accuracy of the descriptions. The results surprised and intrigued TDK's producers, sound supervisors and other employees. TDK employees began staying after the live show to ask me to tell them more about the Catalog of Human Population. Many of them asked me for information about themselves and their relatives and I gave them the information. In December of 2005, I appeared on another Moscow TV channel, Capital.

23. Beginning October 2005, right after my first appearance on TV, people started contacting us through our website. People were asking for information from the Catalog of Human Population about themselves and their relatives and acquaintances. These were regular Russian citizens and also citizens of other former Soviet Union countries (Ukraine, Byelorussia, Baltic Republics). Russian speaking residents of Europe and America were also contacting us. These people were offering their sponsorship in exchange for information. Since we were always finding our own financial means to support our research (thanks to the fact that the information from the Catalog of Human Population has vast practical application), we decided to start working again. At the beginning of 2006, when Andrey started feeling significantly better, we came back to the decoding of "Shan Hai Jing". Soon, we had a line of people, who requesting information and we worked a lot. We finally got some money after Andrey was ill for a while and we were able to pay off our debts. We were particularly pleased, since people who ordered our materials, started giving us their grateful and enthusiastic feedback. They were writing to us that, finally, thanks to the discovery of the Catalog of Human Population, made by Andrey, they found themselves, they got the opportunity to live a full, normal, happy, lives and most importantly, theirs, as opposed to somebody else's, life; that they found mutual understanding with those who they were willing to be with, that they built relationships, acquired true freedom, independence, self-confidence, health, and many other things. We were happy that, finally, the Catalog of Human Population found its direct application: it was used for the good of people, for their development, for self-perfection, for solving problems. We were also happy that the Catalog of Human Population was not being used by well-fed State Duma deputies or officials, as it was in the past, not by members of Special Forces or by politicians for their dirty affairs, but by common people.

24. On March 23rd 2006, the show cancelled my next scheduled appearance which was supposed to take place on April 6th. The editors could not give me a clear explanation as to why it happened. They sounded like they were hiding the truth and gave a vague answer about changing management.

25. A little bit later, in the summer of 2006, bookstores started giving us our books back; and again, it was despite buyers' clear interest towards them. The bookstores' explanations for the returns resembled that of TDK.

26. The small period of prosperity that allowed us to further our work on the Catalog of Human Population toward the end of 2005 and in the first half of 2006 ended during the summer of 2006. In addition to the problems with the TV programs and bookstores, we started having new problems in the summer of 2006. Somebody tried to destroy our website. Then we had problems with our bank accounts. For example, my Savings Bank's department head asked me to close my account without any reasons and absolutely groundlessly. Our communication connections began to falter too: emails did not reach us or would get lost; phone calls would not come through etc. We stopped receiving messages from our website. I was never invited to appear on TV again, on various pretexts, despite my offers. The denials only occurred after Andrey stopped supplying analysis to the FSB. Periodicals stopped accepting our articles about the Catalog of Human Population as well despite previously and gladly receiving many articles from us before. For example, Andrey's articles had been regularly published about the Catalog of Human Population in such Moscow magazines as "Oracle," "Fortitude," and others. For example, the magazine "Questions of Psychology" chose not publish our article despite the fact that it was compiled in accordance with the strict format required for scientific articles. The denials only began occurring after we stopped helping Colonel Polunchuk  Additionally, although Andrey had the respect and cooperation of top Russian scientists when he worked at the Far Eastern Institute, such as famous sinoligist and a translator from the Chinese language Vladimir Vyacheslavovich Malyavin  and famous sinoligist, scientist-orientalist, professor Anatoliy Evgenievich Lukyanov, the academic and scientific circles began to avoid us or only reluctantly speak with us beginning in 2005. Nobody was preventing Andrey in his attempts to talk about his discovery before he turned his back on the FSB. Before Andrey refused to further cooperate with the FSB, Andrey was invited to speak at scientific conferences and round-tables. For example, when he worked at the International Academy of Anthropology in 1997, he was asked to present at the First Russian Philosophical Congress and he presented "Human Being-Philosophy-Humanism" (Volume VII, The Philosophy of Human Problems) edited by corresponding member RAO Verbickaya, L.A and by associate professor Sokolova B.G., Saint-Petersburg, 1997). In 2002, Andrey also presented another one of his papers at the international conference

International Conference of Prospects of preservation and development of Uniform Planetary Civilization. Culture, Ecology, Cosmos», Moscow, 2002 on the discovery of the Catalog of Human Population.

27. On my end, I began to have problems in the academic circles with regarding to work on the Catalog of Human Population. I wanted to write my candidate's and doctoral dissertations on the Catalog of Human Population for my postgraduate study but the faculty's initial great interest transformed into rejection for unexplained reasons. The only thing I was able to do in Moscow academic circles was to conduct a series of lectures about the Catalog of Human Population in the II Moscow Medical Institute through an acquaintance, epidemiologist <name>, who was teaching there and who gave me access on an unofficial basis to his student audience. Similar attempts in other scientific institutions in Moscow did not succeed. I also tried to contact scientists from other countries but did not receive any responses. I believe the FSB monitored our mailboxes, physical and electronic, and such information or responses were withheld from me. I believe this occurred because I discovered that my Gmail account was hacked and all of the incoming email was being redirected to an unknown site.

28. In 2006 we also started having problems with our website. No matter where comments about the discovery of the Catalog of Human Population would appear, someone would instantly show up and would start defaming it in a rough and rude manner. Quite often, we or others, who were announcing our discovery would get blocked on forums and the information about the Catalog of Human Population would get deleted. We were really surprised at that time as to where such aversion to this information and such outrageous responses were coming from. I believe the FSB was responsible for what was happening online with our website and forum. Significantly later, I came across an article, which was describing the FSB's methods of Internet campaigns on Russian forums; I instantly recognized the familiar style: open rudeness, insults, threats, breaking into mailboxes etc. As a result of the attacks online and to protect the credibility of the work for those who remained interested in the benefits and discoveries available through the Catalog of Human Population, we closed the forum. However, even after we closed the forum, these unknown people didn't stop their attacks. Some unknown people started bothering our sponsors with phone calls and strange letters. Nobody could understand where these people were able to obtain their emails and phone numbers. We believe the FSB was using threats and intimidation in an attempt to get us to stop our work. Then, most probably, the same strangers started writing to Andrey and me in an insulting manner. These strangers were trying to obtain materials from the Catalog of Human Population. They were literally demanding that we give them this information. And although they were ready to pay for offered information,

their request was done in such a rude manner, that we flatly refused to give them this information from the Catalog of Human Population. We decided that it would be better for us to lose money than communicate with them.

29. The emails, e-blasts, forum insults, and letters were not the end of the attacks. One night, unfortunately I don't remember the date, when I was working I heard the door bell ringing. I saw a person [his name and names of other suspected employees of FSB from A. D. Polonchuk's group are provided after the text (under endnote [1])] through the peephole. He told me, as he stood behind the closed door, that he was the one, who got blocked on the forum and that he was demanding access to the information from the Catalog of Human Population. I refused to talk to him. Then, he started ringing the doorbell repeatedly, knocking on the door, while shouting out insults. I didn't call the police at that time, since my metal door was durable enough to sustain the pressure of this stranger. Most importantly, I had more important things to do – my work. This incident, of course, was not the only one when somebody was trying to distract us from what we do.

30. Approximately at the same time (the end of 2006), I started having problems with my health as well. Fatigue, headaches and stomachaches were bothering me, and even preventing me from doing my work. I began to suffer from fever almost every day; 37.2-37.4 Celsius (98.96-99.32F). It was very difficult for me to work. Having confirmed that this fever was not connected to any inflammation, colds and so on, I saw a doctor. Doctors conducted a complete medical checkup, yet they couldn't identify the reason for the everyday sub febrile temperature.

31. Around the same time period, Andrey started feeling bad again. However, at that time we thought that this ailment was due to overwork. Although some disorders, for example Andrey's sudden chronic rhinitis, in our opinion, were not connected to fatigue from work.

32. A little bit later, in 2007, they found a series of benign tumors in my body. I was extremely surprised since I have never had anything like that before. I didn't have any serious chronic illnesses, I was exercising every day for several hours, I was following a certain diet and I was living a healthy life style, since Andrey's and my research work was not easy and it demanded good health.

33. In 2007 we were still working on decoding programs to create the complete version of the Catalog of Human Population, but we started thinking about a break.

34. Our break was short lived because at the end of 2008, Kate Bazilevsky, a U.S. citizen with Russian origins contacted us and got the materials about herself and invited us to her home in San Diego, California. We agreed after some hesitation because she was interested in further communication with

us. Kate first ordered the materials about one of her acquaintances and then about herself. According to her, all the information was incredibly true, although we lived on different continents and never met her or her boyfriend in person. Being impressed with the possibilities of this technology, Kate told her close friend <name> about the Catalog of Human Population. <Name> could not believe for a long time in the validity of the Catalog, despite Kate's enthusiastic feedback. However, one day she decided to try it and contacted us to get information about herself. She received the decoding of one of the manipulation modes of her sub-type structure. The next day <name> decided to get the decryption of her individual program and all other materials about herself. In 2009, the relationship between Andrey, Kate and I became friendly as well as professional. We corresponded regularly and talked over Skype. Kate told us a lot about San Diego. She lived in Ocean Beach and was telling us that her house was located four blocks away from the ocean. She described her home as a vacation destination and we became interested in her home for health restoration.

35. In the summer of 2009 there was another event that happened: Andrey moved in with me in the apartment located at ... (Before that, he was regularly visited me for 2 to 3 days at a time; however, we lived in separate apartments).

36. At that time, our health was becoming worse. Other than the above-mentioned disorders, in the summer of 2009, they discovered a cyst in Andrey's jaw. Previously, doctors had found a cyst in my ovary and one may consider the cysts to be coincidental; however, medical sources insist that the effect of poisoning substances can lead, among other things, to cyst formation.

## First Trip to The United States

37. As our health declined, we seriously started thinking about vacation options. Kate persuaded us to visit her in Summer 2009 by invitation. I applied for an American tourist visa first and I got it in September 2009.

38. In October of 2009, without Andrey, I came to the United States for 2 weeks. We wanted to confirm that the location where Kate was inviting us to was suitable for restoring our health. We were planning on resting for more than 1 month.

39. I stayed at Kate's place in San Diego for 2 weeks in October/November 2009. The location was indeed wonderful. We had a great time. Kate, <name> and I traveled around sightseeing; I had a chance to rest for a little bit and came back to Moscow delighted with my visit.

## Second Trip to The United States

40. Andrey and I decided that we would rest and restore our health in San Diego. In January of 2010, Andrey got a 2-year tourist visa from the embassy of the United States in Moscow.

41. On February 2, 2010, Andrey and I came to America together. At Kate's invitation, we stayed with her at...

42. After six months, our health had improved greatly. However, both of us were sick for the first 2-3 months (we suspected that our suitcases with all the clothing were poisoned in the Russian airport). For example, both of us had severe colds for 1.5 months. Andrey had pain in his ears and I had unusual skin rash and pink scabs that would burst out, fester and wouldn't heal for a long time. However, despite all of it, at the end of the 4th month of us being in the United States, we both not only swam in the ocean every day, but also played tennis almost every day.

## Return to Moscow

43. On August 2, 2010, Andrey and I went back to Moscow. As soon as we arrived, we started feeling bad again, although we hoped it was just the pangs of acclimatization. However, after 2 months of feeling bad and there was no recovery in sight. All our disorders returned. Not only did the conditions return, but they multiplied and strengthened.

44. At some point, complaining to each other again about our ailments, we discovered with surprise that we had the same symptoms. For example, we both felt really weak, incredibly sleepy (we could sleep up to 18 hours per day at that time), we both had some strange spasms in our entire body, constant dryness of the mouth, constant heaviness in the chest, periodical nausea, bloating, and pain after each food intake etc. In general, it seemed that both of us were in the semiconscious state all the time. Having noticed it and the big difference in our health condition after we came back to our homeland, we suspected that something was wrong. Previously, we had believed that our poor health might be attributed to exhaustion or getting older but upon the reoccurrence of intensified symptoms after our return to Russia, we were left to believe in the only logical conclusion, that we were being poisoned.

45. At the end of November of 2010, our health became really bad. In addition to the abovementioned symptoms, our eyesight significantly decreased. I also was unable to focus and everything was blurry even though I have never had problems with my sight before and never wore glasses previously. We had problems with breathing, heartbeat, finger tremors (Andrey's thumb would also get numb), bitterness in our mouths, and overall foul taste. Also both of us had spasms in our stomachs and rather painful bloating after eating. We both started having problems with

our skin. We both had some strange spots, crusts on our arms or legs (we have pictures), and Andrey also suffered from skin boils. He was also complaining that there was something hot flowing in his veins. We also had disorders with coordination of movements and I also even had speech impairment, which I have never had before. Our memory and thinking functions became significantly worse. We couldn't concentrate. In addition to this, both of us had extremely dry skin, our hair started falling out, and our nails would break. Andrey 's nails, for example, folded inside in a strange manner.

46. The scariest thing that happened to our health occurred in November 2010. Andrey, for the first time in his life, started having suffocation fits. The first time it happened at night while he was sleeping. When it happened, he jumped out of bed all of a sudden and ran to the kitchen. He told me later that if he didn't take some ice from the fridge, put it on his throat and sit next to the fan, he most probably would have suffocated because the spasm that squeezed his throat was very strong.

47. After this incident we tried to seek medical help. On December 1, 2010, the therapist Klochkova, Olga Leonidovna from the outpatient clinic Aerolife, after hearing about our symptoms (we came to see her together) suspected that both of us were being poisoned. One of the indices in Andrey's blood analysis revealed an extremely high level of the choline esterase which strengthened the doctor's opinion. We later found out from medical summaries that the change in the choline esterase level could be connected to the poisoning from the organophosphorous compounds when using weaponized poisonous substances. The doctor suspected poisoning but didn't know by what or how so she suggested we see a toxicologist. On December 12, 2010, she gave us referrals to several places since she didn't know who would agree to treat us.

48. Andrey, <name> (she started having ailments similar to ours after visiting us at my apartment where Andrey and I lived) and I went to see toxicologists. In December of 2010 we tried to get a consultation in the Sklifosofsky Institute. However, we were prescribed treatments with enemas and activated carbon. They didn't tell us what to do with the suffocation fits and didn't explain why these fits were happening. One toxicologist openly humiliated us, suggesting seeing a psychiatrist. Another more gentle denial to treat us was the following: a toxicologist, after listening to our complaints, declared that these symptoms confused him so much that he was unable to determine what we were poisoned with. He told us we had been poisoned by "some weird mixture" and "for the first time I can't understand what is happening here, I've never seen anything like that before." As a result, we left again without any diagnosis, medication, recommendations, or explanations as to what was happening. We ended up in an extremely difficult situation because there

are only a few toxicologists in Moscow, which the general public might use and we went to all of them and they all refused to treat us.

49. Unfortunately, in December 2010 when we sent to see the different toxicologists we didn't have any official documented proof to support poisoning. We only got it in January 2011.

50. Later, Andrey and I learned why the toxicologists refused to treat us. In a conversation with my acquaintance, a medical doctor named *<name>*, told me that when he ran into a non-traditional case of chronic poisoning symptoms, which were not connected to a job at some hazardous manufacturing plant or to participation in the act of war, he preferred not to deal with patients like that. In response to my questions as to why it was happening, he told me that doctors tried to escape getting wrapped up into dark stories. In response to my questions as to what stories he was talking about, Dr. *<name>* stated that doctors considered that when it was unclear as to who poisoned these patients and with what substances, they were either connected to criminal groups or the Special Forces of the Russian Federation. According to him, none of the doctors wanted to have problems so they refused to involve themselves in such cases. Also, Dr. *<name>* explained that toxicologists treated either acute poisoning, to which our case didn't relate, or they treated chronic toxic exposure at some manufacturing plant. We left without treatment because the three of us did not work at such plants, nor was the poisoning acute. I asked but Dr. *<name>* didn't answer my question as to what we were supposed to do. He honestly stated that he didn't know what we should do since he was a therapist, not a toxicologist. For the first time after many years of helping my family and I, he refused to examine us or prescribe any medication.

51. At the end of December 2010, Andrey and I clearly understood that we couldn't find medical help anywhere in Moscow. His fits not only continued but also became stronger. They started happening on a daily basis. They were really strong and life threatening. I thought that any time, one of his fits would be his last. We felt in desperate need to do something and it was absolutely clear that if we didn't help ourselves, nobody would help us.

52. We started looking for information on poisonous substances and poison treatment methodologies on our own. We studied a huge volume of special literature. As a result, we found something that worked. We started taking supplements. We took calcium chloride several times a day, glucose, Meksidol pills, magnium sulphate (inside and adding it to baths), certain essential oils like lavender oil which helped with spasms, and other substances. However, all the remedies that we found didn't solve the problem of Andrey's suffocation fits. He still had to jump out in the middle of the night, put on ice and sit in front of open windows for hours. Due to these fits we had to sleep in a very cold premises (at negative twenties Celsius below freezing with open windows throughout the apartment).

53. The remedies we used helped with our symptoms. We went through kilometers of patches soaked in essential oils which we applied as compresses to our bodies; liters of calcium chloride and magnesium, kilograms of glucose, and piles of pills for breakfast, lunch and dinner. When I was buying yet another batch of all the remedies in one Moscow pharmacy in the quantity sufficient for both of us and our relatives who were getting poisoned with us, the pharmacist actually asked me if I was making the purchase on behalf of a pharmacy.

54. At the end of December 2010, we arranged for something else to save us. We examined all the probable areas in our apartment, where these poisonous substances could be placed, pulverized, or spilled. At that point, we didn't have time to think as to who did it to us or why. Our concern was not to die. We removed the woolen carpet from the room. The carpet had a strange smell despite the fact that after we came back from the United States we dry-cleaned it. We wrapped it up in tight bags and put it on the balcony for further expert examination. Later we threw away our sofa and our bed mattress. We also had to throw away a completely new natural merino blanket since we couldn't wash it and at that time we were afraid to dry clean it. We had to throw away a lot of other things too. What I could wash and not throw away I did, including curtains, pillows, blankets, sheets, and clothing. In addition, I thoroughly cleaned the entire living premises with ammonia. *<name>* brought us an air mattress so we wouldn't have to sleep on the floor.

55. We continued to receive confirmation that of our hypothesis that someone was poisoning us. On December 31st, 2010, New Year's Eve, I went outside to take out the garbage. We had problems with locking our metal front door at the time and this time one part of the lock fell off. I picked it up and I discovered that it was the metal plate, which was covering a portion of the lock. Most probably this plate was attached with one bolt, which fell off. I asked Andrey for help. When trying to fix the lock, to our surprise, we discovered that the plate which fell off had covered the inside of the lock itself, which was broken! We discovered big cracks on each side of the lock, which couldn't appear on their own. The discovery that the front door to our apartment was broken into became the last fact, which completed the picture. It became very clear: somebody was persecuting Andrey and I. Moreover, this somebody was trying to kill us using some poison, which they have put into our apartment.

56. Of course one could assume that we got poisoned outside of our apartment. However, since we came back from the United States, Andrey and I had not visited anybody or spent any significant period of time in any location other than our apartment. We didn't go out much because we felt too sick to visit anybody. We were inviting our relatives and acquaintances

to visit us. We concluded that we were being poisoned only in our apartment and that the persecutors were responsible for the broken lock.

57. However, despite all the facts, this picture looked unreal. We were peaceful people and we lived in peaceful times. Andrey and I started looking for similar cases in different sources in order to not feel paranoid or rely too heavily on our fears. We found several similar cases of other people being poisoned in Russia or even specifically by the FSB or KGB. For example, Russian doctor Baranov V.V. and his wife, scientist-chemist, Baranova T.A who escaped from agents from former KGB to the United States and who currently live in Los Angeles, accuse Russian special forces on their website (http://www.baranovfamily.org/index.html) in widespread secret use of special substances against peaceful people. These researchers, who became victims of KGB terrorism, not only know the problem that we had to deal with, but also, being experts in chemistry and medicine, give out detailed information about how this process takes place. Unfortunately, we found a lot of things in their description, which almost exactly illustrated what was happening to us.

58. After familiarizing ourselves with some materials, it became clear: anybody who was connected to the information about the actual V.V. Putin's actions were killed or disappeared without any trace. There was also information found that Putin's preferred method of eliminating people who were out of his favor was poisoning, which was the only method of killing, when a person is dying as if from natural causes such as pulmonary or brain edema, heart attack, stroke or any other common disease. This method was implemented by Russian Special Forces. Putting two and two together, Andrey and I understood that the Russian Special Forces were poisoning us.

59. From reading different publications, it became clear that the FSB was one of the few organizations in Russia, which operated outside of the law and only obeyed the orders of former Russian President V.V. Putin. Clearly, the FSB alliance and service to Putin and his illegal orders is comparable to that of a mafia alliance. (The former KGB is nothing else but a legalized group of criminals. This organization doesn't serve Russian people, but only its master, Putin. There are a lot of articles, which state that the Russian former president Putin is a killer. For example, Timothy Naegele in "Russia's Putin Is A Killer" states Putin is as sinister and evil as Joseph Stalin, Adolf Hitler and Mao Tse-tung, as well as that he is a ruthless killer of his own people and others, and of the human spirit. In addition, he defines Putin absolutely and directly as a mafia leader. Naegele further lists facts of cruelty, which Putin and his Ex-KGB lackeys brought upon Russia and other countries.

60. The information found in multiple informational sources matched Andrey's personal experience and confirmed his opinion that the FSB, SVR,

and GRU act as gangs of criminals who can do whatever they want to whomever they want. Andrey learned about how the groups worked while communicating with Colonel Polonchuk and the other FSB agents over approximately five years. I think that only because of his experience and special knowledge we were able to surmise that something extraordinary and life-threatening was happening to us. If Andrey hasn't learned for himself that FSB agents were engaged in murders, perhaps he, and all the more so I, would have never thought that the defenders of public order were capable of killing peaceful citizens in broad daylight. And then our killers would finish their case for certain.

## Andrey Tells Me the Full Story of His Involvement Assisting The FSB

61. Andrey told me the story about his meetings and communication with FSB in greater detail toward the end of 2010 because of what was happening to us.

62. Andrey told me he met the colonel of Foreign Intelligence Service (department of FSB) Andrey Dmitrievich Polonchuk, not long before Putin's election as Russian President (June-July of 1999). Polonchuk found the information about the Catalog of Human Population research in the magazine Power of Spirit where Andrey published the article "Myths or Psyche structure?" in co-authorship with one of his acquaintances from ITAR TASS V. Fedoruk.

63. They met in the following way: A man, who introduced himself as Andrey Dmitrievich Polonchuk. He said that he was interested in the Power of Spirit article and the Catalog of Human Population and he offered to meet. Polonchuk also asked Andrey whether he had information about him personally. Andrey responded that he would do it for him as a special request because he had not yet done the corresponding program using the Catalog of Human Population yet and Polonchuk asked in a very polite manner for him to bring these materials to the meeting.

64. The meeting occurred not too far from MHAT theatre, at the boulevard. The information which Polonchuk requested was the exact decoding of his individual program from the Catalog of Human Population. Andrey brought the decoding to the meeting and gave it to him. Polonchuk was very impressed with the materials he received because of its accuracy in describing him. They parted ways after this.

65. According to Andrey, Polonchuk organized their further meetings over the phone. They met in different cafes and restaurants including café Pyramid near the movie theatre, Pushkin at the Pushkin Square, a Chinese restaurant at the new MHAT building, and a café near the metro stop Ohotnyj Ryad. At first, Polunchuk was requesting exclusively personal

information from the Catalog: about his relatives, son, wife and acquaintances. He justified his requests stating that he had to be certain that the technology of estimating the structure of human psyche, which Andrey developed, was really working. Once he was done with his verification, Polonchuk announced that he had no objections or complaints about the information Andrey was provided him.

66. Right after this verification ended, in the summer of 2000, during one of their next meetings, Polonchuk introduced himself as an agent of the FSB. He showed Andrey his identification as a Colonel in the Foreign Intelligence Service.

67. Polonchuk asked Andrey to prepare analytical materials about V.V. Putin, who then-recently (May 2000) came to power. The goals of this analysis were the following: find out if the new Russian President was temporary or not, how long Putin would stay at power, which personal financial capital he had, where he kept it, and how he used it.

68. Andrey has never conducted such analytical work prior to this case, although as a researcher, he found this request rather interesting. In addition, this work paid well. (As a note, in 2000 the average salary of Russian citizens was $83 per month, and Andrey got offered $..,000 for this work). Andrey was exclusively conducting scientific research at that time and he didn't have stable income and he needed money. He agreed to Polonchuk's offer.

69. Andrey completed this analytical work, received the promised fee, and gave the materials about Putin to Polonchuk. Andrey told me that Polonchuk was disappointed in the results of Andrey's research because Polunchuk and his bosses, a group of his colleagues from FSB, were hoping that Putin would not remain at power for long and that Putin would be replaced in one to two months. This group most probably counted on joining someone who would replace the new President. Although Polonchuk never openly stated that he was against Putin, based on all the signs, it was exactly so. The research about the personality of the new Russian President pointed out that their hopes had no chance of realizing. The analysis clearly indicated that Putin not only would occupy the President's chair for long, but he was planning on building the power system covering the entire Eurasian region. Putin would be able to find financial means for this global project. And he would find it by using FSB as the repressive apparatus to illegally take money from people who were transferring their capital abroad or accumulating it in the territories of the Russian Federation.

70. Despite the fact that Andrey upset this group of FSB agents with his predictions, a little bit later Polonchuk not only enthusiastically thanked Andrey for his analytical work, but also gave him a bonus. The bonus was in the additional amount of $...,000. Andrey was really surprised by the bonus and enthusiastic thanks of Poluchuk. Polonchuk explained that Andrey

seriously helped him and his bosses to orient them in the situation and correctly adjust their behavior by absolutely and exactly calculating who Putin was and what kind of policy he would implement. Thanks to Andrey's analytical work, this FSB group was not only not fired or worse, but instead most probably they were able to advance in their careers. However, Andrey was still really surprised by the generous bonus. Since, according to Andrey, FSB agents were never generous in the past with regard to payment for services.

71. Andrey didn't know that his analytical work would make him target for elimination. Andrey didn't know that people like him, people who were conducting such predictions for the FSB, didn't live long. And people, who possessed information compromising to the FSB generals and colonels (in this case Andrey had information that Polonchuk, his bosses and other colleagues had been part of an anti-Putin alignment within the FSB) were eliminated even faster.

72. It is necessary to note that, as Andrey explained to me later, money and research curiosity did not form the basic reason for his agreement to fulfill orders for the FSB. Andrey hoped his work for the FSB would result in large investments and a new laboratory for his research. He reminded me that he has already discussed with Polunchuk the idea of obtaining funding for a laboratory, which would attract specialists to expedite the creation of the complete version of the Catalog of Human Population. Andrey's existing laboratory was insufficient for such a level of research and all the more so, since there was not enough financing. Polonchuk expressed his interest in financing this project at some point. This mere fact was the only reason he was persuaded to conduct this research and give the information from the Catalog of Human Population to Polonchuk. According to Andrey, he knew that Special Forces agents had large monetary funds.

73. His meeting with Polonchuk was characterized by long breaks. Polonchuk would usually disappear for 2-6 months. He would always call himself and only for the purpose of setting up a meeting. Andrey had no reason to call Polonchuk since Polonchuk had 2-3 phone numbers at the same time and he would change them every one and a half to two months; the only connection they had was Polonchuk's orders. Polonchuk always appear with the same offer: place another order for FSB and make some money, while the issue of opening the laboratory is still being decided.

74. Month after month, Polonchuk prolonged the decision in regards to financing the laboratory. He kept telling Andrey "tomorrow" and would offer to place another order. Andrey was forced to agree in order not to lose the opportunity to solve his research and financial problems.

75. According to Andrey, 3 years of his research and analytical work for FSB ended in the following manner. With the hope that Polonchuk would soon redeem his promise in regards to the laboratory, Andrey was fulfilling a

series of orders. Given that it's been 11 years, Andrey didn't remember dates and research subjects. He also didn't mention the names of people who Polonchuk introduced him to. These customers would never introduce themselves. Andrey only knew that all of them were Polonchuk's colleagues at FSB.

76. For the period beginning from the first transfer of information about Putin (summer of 2000 to summer of 2003) Andrey, for example, completed the order for the Antiterrorist Center, where Polonchuk worked at that time. This center was organized as Putin's idea and it was located in Moscow at Old Square. Andrey was asked to complete the theoretical and practical parts on Terrorism. He conducted research in the suggested subject area and he gave completed materials to Polonchuk. That meeting took place around metro station Novoslobodskaya where Polonchuk lived. All the analytical materials that Andrey prepared for Polonchuk were deleted from Andrey's computer himself. However, Andrey managed to save one of the documents titled "Terrorism Concepts," confirming his authorship in these developments.

77. Andrey also completed a few other orders. He gave analytical materials, which were created on the basis of the Catalog of Human Population about the personalities of the owner of the weaving factory in the city of Ivanovo and of the governor of the Primorye Territory. He also developed the election campaign strategy for the future governor of Moscow District and the President of the Republic of Sakha (Yakutia).

78. Andrey and Polonchuk's business relations became worse after Andrey refused to conduct research on one Canadian businessman who sold dental equipment. Polonchuk's task was to recruit this businessman for nefarious ends, to in fact spy on behalf of the FSB, and if he declined, to either illegally take his money or eliminate him. The reason Andrey refused to fulfill this order was quite natural: he did not want to participate, even indirectly, in murdering people. Andrey thought at that time that Polonchuk had a calm attitude towards Andrey's refusal.

79. 2-3 months after Andrey refused to give information about the Canadian, in the summer of 2003, Polonchuk called Andrey and offered to meet in one of the usual places. At this meeting, Polonchuk offered Andrey to sign documents showing Andrey's official collaboration with FSB. Andrey strongly declined. Again, as Andrey thought, Polonchuk had a calm attitude towards this rejection. This meeting was the last between the two men.

80. Through our conversations together remembering the events of the past, we concluded that FSB persecution of us began, as they say, not yesterday, because exactly then, in the summer of 2003, Andrey became ill for the first time although he was perfectly healthy before then. And in the summer of 2003, I entered his life, and, unfortunately, I became a direct witness to these problems with his health. We understood that we were

getting poisoned not only after our return to Russia from the United States in August of 2010, but significantly earlier.

81. Several factors have led us to believe that the special forces of the FSB or a group of persons in collusion with Colonel Polunchuk are positioned to kill us if we had remained in Russia of if we return to Russia. These factors include, but are not limited to, the manner and method of the poisoning included sophisticated compounds mixtures (not completely identifiable in trace), the manner of how our apartment was broken into; the tapping of our phones; the hacking of our computers, the refusal of local law enforcement agencies to assist us. Moreover, these attempts against Andrey and I have not been related to any criminal activity since neither Andrey nor I, nor our relatives, acquaintances, colleagues, or anyone else within our circle of friends or acquaintances, are involved in any criminal activities and are not participants in any criminal schemes. We believe we were targeted because of our work on the Catalog of Human Population, and specifically because of Andrey's refusal to provide the FSB with Catalog of Human Population-based information that would be used for harm.

82. During 2003 and 2004, Andrey did not feel well on multiple occasions. It was strange to observe that this strong and healthy man, who was an athlete in the past (Combat Wushu), a person who was exercising on a daily basis for 30 years, was complaining about weakness and some unexplainable pain. Andrey himself was perplexed as to what was happening to him, he said that he had never suffered from any serious illnesses. By the summer of 2004, he started having problems even when he was walking. I became seriously concerned and suggested that Andrey see a doctor. Not inclined to see doctors and take medication, he refused at first. But I insisted and on August 19th, 2004, a doctor from the Outpatient Clinic under the Department of Defense for the City of Moscow examined Andrey. The examination's result was terrifying: computer tomography showed that Andrey had a delaminating abdominal aortic aneurysm. Due to the mortal danger of such a disorder, he was hospitalized. Soon thereafter, they performed aortic bypass surgery and placed a stent in Andrey's body. The source of the delaminating abdominal aortic aneurysm remained unknown to doctors and us.

83. According to our calculations and looking back over the past several years, we know now that the FSB began to slowly poison to death Andrey as soon as he refused to fulfill the FSB order and denied the official collaboration with this organization. Right after these two events he started having ailments, which rather quickly led to Andrey's aneurism, which came from nowhere, and to the loss of working-capacity.

84. All the more so since it was very simple to poison him, as Andrey lived alone in his apartment and it wasn't difficult for an FSB special killing team to put the poisonous substances in his apartment when Andrey was out.

85. As our study of similar cases indicated, the style of poisoning that we experienced matched completely and exactly the style used by the killers from the special forces of Russian Federation. The examined materials supported that the method, which was chosen to kill Andrey and I was "unapparent murder;" murder which could not be ever discovered by anybody. It turned out that they were disabling my common law husband and I for several years, and they were depriving us of our working capacity by regularly poisoning us with small doses of toxic chemical substances.

86. However, it became evident that our inability to work was only an interim result for our murderers. The logical end of their persecution could only be one – our death. And, only natural death. Andrey's suffocation fits clearly demonstrated what kind of end his murderers were leading him to.

87. The analysis of the poisoning issue and chronology of events gave answer to the question as to why, at that time, I didn't have significant health disorders, which Andrey had. Even with similar symptoms between two of us, in general, his health condition was significantly worse than mine. For example, I didn't have those horrible spasms, which, as iron clutches, were squeezing his throat and chest almost every night, putting his life on the verge of death. I didn't have lead and cadmium in my blood. (Although, as medical sources state, lead and cadmium are accumulated not in the blood but they have a property of depositing in bones, internal organs and so on; and since I checked only my blood, the result of this test, by no means, doesn't guarantee the lack of heavy metals in my body). In addition, the results of Andrey's spirometry established that his bronchial efficiency dropped by 70% and everything was much better with my respiration: I was just suffering from constant pressure in my chest and unstoppable dry cough.

88. At the beginning, this difference confused us; however, soon we realized that prior to us living together, killers from FSB were not really interested in me. Andrey was their target. And that's how it was, based on our calculations, from 2003-2009, prior to Andrey moving in with me. Only after we started living in the same apartment, they started poisoning both of us.

89. Yet, based on my strange ailments, which began in 2006, they were periodically dealing with me as well. However, most probably they were interested in me only because I was the owner of the apartment where Andrey often stayed. As we found out from the special literature, such chronic poisoning requires periodic "renewals"; and it became more difficult to poison Andrey in his apartment since at some point his mom and son began living there with him. He was visiting me regularly and they could sneak in to my apartment without any problems (because we don't know how long ago they cracked my door) and plant the next dose of poisons.

90. In addition, almost right after Andrey moved in with me in July of 2009, I almost immediately (in October) went to the United States. And in 3 months (In February 2011) we went there together.

91. Thus, the period of Andrey's regular poisoning was approximately 8 years (2003-2011), and mine, if we wouldn't count one-time actions, when I would get poisoned for company's sake, around 1-1.5 years. That's why we have such a big difference in our current states of health. As medical sources state, toxic substances are accumulated in the body from one time to another when there is chronic poisoning. Obviously, Andrey's body accumulated much more poison during these years than mine.

92. On January 4, 2011, we contacted the police as soon as we finally realized what was happening to us. As the owner of the apartment, I reported a crime in connection to the discovery of the break in the door. The police accepted my statement and I have a document proving it. And they took my lock to conduct expert examination. However, on January 13, 2011, prior to getting the results of this expert examination, I got denied of request to initiate criminal proceedings.

93. Right after that (around January 15, 2011, I don't remember exactly) we called in experts from the Moscow Center for Hygiene and Epidemiology. We wanted to find out the condition of our premises and we also hoped that if they found something bad and something out of the ordinary, FSB would be unable to force such a large organization to substitute the results of the examination. Partially, our calculations were correct.

94. Upon conducting three examinations, the experts discovered chemical substances in the quantity, which was hazardous for health and life. They examined the air in the apartment and the air near the carpet, which was initially in the middle of the room and which was later was taken out to the balcony; they also examined the air near the bed, in the closet, and in the hallway. Excess of the maximum permissible concentration (MPC) in the living premises (room) amounted to: the concentrations of dibutyl phthalate was almost 10 times higher than MPC (carpet examination, which was taken out of the room to the balcony due to the strange smell in the room); the concentration of styrene was 5.5 times higher than MPC (near the bed); the concentration of formaldehyde was 3 times higher than MPC (also near the bed); and the concentration of volatile components of the aromatic mixture was 34 times higher than MPC. Air probes in the closet revealed that the concentration of styrene was 8 times higher than MPC, concentration of naphthalene was 7 times higher than MPC and the concentration of the volatile components of the aromatic mixture was almost 40 times higher.

95. We got this information from the official reports and expert findings (as of January 17th and January 26th of 2011). Out apartment was officially found uninhabitable after they found the concentration of some unknown

elements (which were called "aromatic hydrocarbons," 40 times higher than normal and other chemical substances in quantities hazardous to life and health.

96. We suspect that there was forgery of the last examination (gas chromatography and mass-spectrometry of the carpet), which we requested at the Moscow Center for Hygiene and Epidemiology on January 28th 2011 (carpet sample). We concluded that the forgery was due to, firstly, the fact that we had to wait for a long time for the results. At first, we were told over the phone that the experts got some strange, in their opinion, readings and that they couldn't identify what was found. Secondly, when I called them again in regards to the delay of the results, the head of the laboratory, Andrey Yulievich Poltorackiy, told me the following: "We have big problems because of you, we have an inspection!" Thirdly, the inspectors demanded, for some reason, to withdraw the results of the prior examination. According to Poltorackiy, they demanded it based on the assumption that the prior examination was wrong since it was impossible to find the substances, which were found in the living premises. Fourthly, they had already probed the air near the carpet (during the first examination) when they found 10 times higher than normal quantity of dibutyl phthalate so there was no way to hide it unless they took back the initial test. Lastly, simultaneously to the expert analysis, we had also given a carpet sample to our acquaintance chemist, who examined it unofficially in his laboratory and found big quantity of phthalates. Clear discrepancy in the results of three examinations of the same carpet, two of which were conducted by the same organization, plus the demand of returning the results of the initial examination and offer to redo the expert examination (by the way, they offered it for free!) led us instantly to conclude FSB interference because only the FSB is capable of forcing such a large and trustworthy governmental establishment as the Moscow Center for Hygiene and Epidemiology to forge documents and withdraw correct scientific findings.

97. While talking to experts from the Moscow Center for Hygiene and Epidemiology, we found out a lot of information, which was not officially documented. Firstly, we and <name>, who was present during all the expert examinations, witnessed all the seriousness of the experts' confusion as to the results they have obtained. The quantity and the type of substances found in our apartment shocked them. The experts said that it was the first time they came across such conditions in a private apartment. The experts came to the dead end and didn't know how to explain what they'd found. The experts told us the results were not based on the air outside the apartment which they tested, nor could it be connected to furniture in the apartment, and the volatile components of the aromatic mixtures which were 40 times higher than normal could only arise to the same level if there was a one time ejection at a perfumery factory. In response to the question as to whether the substances found in our apartment could be considered

poisonous and whether they were dangerous for our health, all the experts responded the same thing: given fixated levels of 30 to 40 times higher than normal, all these substances can be considered poisonous. The experts recommended escaping the "gas chamber," that's how they referred to our apartment, as soon as possible.

98. We also asked the experts as to how long one had to work on our apartment in order to lead to such hazardous for life conditions. They responded that it would take a long time to achieve such results; and it also required special training on the part of those who were doing it. They also stated that a non-professional would not only ever be able to achieve such results, but also would be under the risk of poisoning himself. And, most certainly, they said, it would be necessary to regularly refresh poisonous substances to maintain certain concentration. However, the experts refused to tell us as to where such specialists could be trained. We knew the answer to this question ourselves, though: such specialists are trained at FSB. These professionals made a "cocktail" of chemical substances in such a way that each "recipe" was tailored for a specific "client" considerate of gender, age, health condition, etc.

99. We also found out that if some of these ordinary, civilian toxicologists or, for example, experts in forensic medicine managed to uncover secret FSB "cocktails" - these people would either vanish without a trace or they would be found dead. When we contacted one expert in forensic medicine telling him that we were getting poisoned by special services, he not only named extremely high price for his services, but he also stated that he would never officially document, for any money in the world, what was found in our apartment.

100. Having discovered such a huge amount of poisonous substances in our apartment, we encountered the problem as to how to clear it out of our bodies on our own, without the help of toxicologists, who practically refused to treat us. We found a method, which cleared the blood from any harmful substances – cascade plasma filtration. This is a procedure of complete blood purification, when the blood is run through special filters, which retain everything harmful and the beneficial substances and the blood itself are returned to the body of a patient.

101. At the end of January 2011 in the American-Russian outpatient clinic Medsi in Moscow, we met with a transfusiologist named Inna Modisovna Mednis, who after hearing our complaints and looking through our medical records, confirmed that such procedure would be indicated. Andrey and I went through this procedure one time. The content of filters after plasma filtration procedure was not encouraging, and Andrey's blood plasma was of such horrific color, that the doctor decided to take a picture of his filter. Inna Modisovna told us she has never seen anything like that before in her life. Due to this result of plasma filtration, she referred Andrey to conduct a

heavy metal panel. The results of these tests shocked all of us: it was found that Andrey had 40% higher of lead content and 20% higher of cadmium! And this was after complete blood purification procedure! Andrey, naturally, asked then: by what percentage of one procedure of cascade plasma filtration lowers the quantity of heavy metals in blood? The doctor responded "by 20-25%." Thus, prior to the first procedure, he could have the concentration of lead at around 60% higher and the concentration of cadmium at around 40% higher than normal. The doctor confirmed these calculations. She also added that even the quantity that was found supported a severe toxic poisoning. In addition, the doctor confirmed the information that we have found in medical literature that lead and cadmium get deposited not in blood but in bones and internal organs. Because it was found that Andrey's blood contained such a huge amount of heavy metals, he went through another cascade blood filtration procedure, and the doctor also recommended repeating this procedure 2 more times or even more.

102. On January 28th 2011, I contacted the police again. I filed another report, attaching official results of the expert examination of our apartment and Andrey's blood results of heavy metal panel. I demanded another investigation based on the discovery of new evidence of the crime against us.

103. We hoped that the police would be able to connect the first police report about the break in the door with the newly discovered evidence that our apartment contained poisonous substances and that my common law husband's blood contained lead and cadmium. The request for investigation was first denied because there was no indication of burglary. We thought that if policemen saw new documents then it would be obvious that someone broke into our apartment not for the purpose of taking something out of it but to plant something – plant the poison.

104. It turned out that our hopes were futile. On February 2011 we got an official denial to our request to initiate criminal investigation in regards to unknown persons who had planted chemical substances in quantity hazardous to human life in our apartment. The basis for this denial didn't tolerate any criticism and it was obviously fabricated. It more resembled idle reasoning and guesses of the police lieutenant Nadirov, Aleksey Yurevich, because they clearly contradicted the conclusions, which experts had made. The conclusions of this policeman actually meant that employees of such a large organization as Moscow Center for Hygiene and Epidemiology were incompetent; and that he, the police lieutenant, on the contrary, was a super-specialist in the questions of chemistry, medicine, and sanitary and epidemiological inspection. It was complete nonsense, of course, but more importantly showed the police were unwilling to protect us.

105. Sometime after this denial in February of 2011, this lieutenant Nadirov, our district police inspector and one person with captain shoulder straps came to visit us. We were surprised: since when district police inspectors were accompanied by higher ranks individuals? This police captain seemed very suspicious due to his behavior and questions he was asking. His behavior more resembled that of an FSB agent. This episode strengthened our opinion that the FSB was working against us.

106. During the period of December 2010 through the end of March 2011, Andrey and I not only came within a whisker of being killed on an everyday basis, but also felt like handcuffed prisoners. For example, beginning December 2010 we stopped going outside together because we were afraid to leave the apartment empty. We would go outside alone only when it was necessary (to buy groceries, visit doctors, etc.).

107. In some time even I practically stopped going outside because of our fear that our suspected future murderers would use more cardinal actions against us.

108. In addition, Andrey and I were forced to stop communicating with our parents and children, since we were afraid that someone would persecute them as well. Our communication circle was really narrow: two acquaintances, who were helping us during these difficult times, who I mentioned above; the therapist Klochkova, O.L, who was trying to treat us somehow and our lawyer <name>. He was helping us with solving issues with police and other governmental agencies, which we were forced to contact. They became sick as well and we suspect poisons were planted on them. For example, <name>'s spirometry detected bronchial obstruction, although her bronchi were normal in the past and she didn't smoke.

109. We stopped using our cell phones because we believed they were not only tapped but were also used as special microphones through which our persecutors were able to follow everything that was happening in our apartment.

110. Having practically stopped using phone connection, we communicated with people through multiple electronic mailboxes. Our acquaintances began noticing strange incidents and malfunctions of mobile and Internet connections. Let me give an example. One day when I woke up, I saw a missed call from <name>. We would keep our phones on at home sometimes in order to at least know who was calling us. However, we would usually leave the phone in the bathroom with running water in order to block all the sounds in the apartment or in some other sound-proof places. I called <name> back but she told me that she didn't call me. We were both confused. Later we resolved it. <Name> told us, that once she hung up after talking to me, she reviewed all her outgoing calls. She discovered not only my number, which she has never dialed, but she also saw as right in front of her eyes this number was getting erased from her phone. Here is another

interesting incident. We unplugged the Internet connection cord from our computer, however the computer was still connected and was able to open up Internet pages. I could offer multiple examples like these.

111. In February of 2011, apparently after our murderers made certain that we not only discovered their plan, but we were also trying to oppose them – we noticed a light on at the attic of the house across. (We have a picture). We asked a policeman, however, he couldn't explain us what it could be. At the same time we noticed that our enemies could get the information not only through the conversations on the cell phones but also through conversations that took place at home. We were able to notice it based on a few indicators. It forced us to think whether some sort of internal sound bugs were installed.

112. The reasons for our persecutors to do so were evident: we practically stopped using our phones, the main building entrance surveillance was problematic, since it was freezing outside, negative 30 degrees Celsius – where would they find the information about us? We were forced to stop talking in the apartment. We always kept a notebook and a pencil on the table in the kitchen and we started communicating with each other and our few acquaintances exclusively in writing, destroying all the notes in a certain manner. (This approach, to run ahead in the chain of events, really helped us that night when we were running out of our apartment – our move was successful and remained unnoticed by our persecutors; and also during the night, when we were forced to run from Russia).

113. Later after this, we started hearing strange noises that were coming from the apartment upstairs where nobody lived for a long time. We also noticed that when we were sleeping with the balcony door open, we would always wake up really beat and Andrey would have a strong suffocation fit.

114. I tried to call the neighbor above, but he wouldn't pick up his phone. Then I contacted the property management, but they didn't know where this neighbor was, they just said that according to their information, this apartment was currently empty. We also discovered a strange stain above our main entrance door; and the similar stain on the kitchen ceiling, which was never there before. We were also alerted with the fact that all houseplants, which we had, turned yellow, dried out and died (we have pictures). All of this led us to conclude that we had to run out of our apartment as soon as possible. All the more so since it was almost impossible to breathe normally in our apartment by that time.

115. On February 11th 2011 late night, without any word, without our phones, taking only minimal necessities with us, Andrey and I left our apartment for good. We moved to the apartment of <name>, who agreed to give us shelter at: ...

116. This arrangement significantly helped Andrey and I to survive. Upon entering <name>'s apartment, we instantly noticed that the atmosphere there was quite different from what we used to have. And we immediately realized the reason: the air in <name>'s apartment was fresh. It didn't contain unpleasant or heavy smells that our apartment had. We caught ourselves thinking that, after a few months of confinement, we practically have forgotten the taste of normal air.

117. It was inappropriate to live in somebody else's apartment for a long time and we couldn't come back anymore, we had no place to live. We had to do something. So we tried to get attention of law enforcement' agencies yet again and to obtain their protection. That is why in the middle of February of 2011, I filed the third statement with the police. I would like to note that the attachments to this statement of all the copies of the documents, which we managed to gather, was so thick that it wouldn't go through the narrow opening in the window of the officer on duty.

118. Andrey and I also contacted journalists, to be exact the reception of Alexandr Lebedev, who is the owner of Novaya Gazeta (New Newspaper). Lebedev responded that he received the materials and they were interesting and that he personally gave it to editors. The editors contacted us over the phone, at one of the times when the phone was on. The reporters said that our information was interesting but they needed some clarifications and that they would call us back. But then we were forced to turn our phones off again and our connection to the entire world was interrupted. Being disconnected, we decided that it was useless to contact other magazines and newspapers. We were forced to stop our attempts of attracting media attention.

119. On March 3rd 2011, without any response from the police, we sent a letter to President A.D. Medvedev and Prime-Minister V.V. Putin. In the middle of March 2011 we received a response from the presidential reception that they directed this case to MVD. As well known, all correspondence from MVD is directed to police, which we have already contacted 3 times by that time. It was the dead end. In regards to Putin's reception, despite the law, which requires this governmental agency to respond to the appeals of all citizens, Andrey and I didn't receive any response to our appeal.

120. I would like to reiterate that all our statements to official agencies were sent with the copies of medical expert examinations. Thus, we presented the proof that Andrey and I were being killed. None of the governmental agencies reacted to our cry for help. I believe it happened because all of these agencies, i.e. police, public prosecutor's office, MVD, Presidential and Prime Minister receptions were not going to interfere in the activity of FSB agents, who were transforming our apartment into premises for slow execution. All of these myrmidons of the law took our killers' side and

covered up their actions. The abovementioned agencies deliberately left Andrey and I, who were sick and absolutely helpless, alone with this special team, which was killing us slowly in the professional and purposeful manner.

121. And this was done despite the existence of the European Convention on Human Rights, based on which, our rights were infringed at least four times: Right to life, Right to security of person, Right to security of residence, and Right to security of personal privacy. Despite the proof that our constitutional rights were violated, none of the governmental agencies reacted to our multiple statements and none of them protected us. (We filed 3 statements only to police, and this is not counting all the statements, requests, complaints, which were filed to other agencies, such as MVD, public prosecutor's office, etc.)

122. In March of 2011, we took last step: we sent a letter to the FSB. However, we didn't wait for their response (and as it turned out later we did the right thing, because FSB supposedly conducted the verification in a very short period of time and based on this verification they denied further investigation); due to all the actions that we took, our lives were even in greater danger than before.

## Fleeing Russia in 2011

123. Once we realized we had nothing else to do, we decided to leave our homeland forever. We exhausted all the chances of survival in this country; the country, where governmental agencies, which were called for protecting its citizens by law, were killing them with impunity.

124. We had to act with no delays. Despite our bad health conditions – Andrey could barely breathe and I wasn't in the best shape either – we had nothing else to do but to escape, leaving everything behind. At that time we had only one visa in our passports – American visa, which was still open from the last visit.

125. We had to leave Russia. It was really difficult to live in the state of permanent fear, not having a possibility of psychological relief day and night, constantly feeling the breath of death behind our backs for a long time. It was very painful to observe how a person, so dear to me, was suffering and to have no chance of helping him. It was unbearable to understand that the killers from FSB could do anything they wanted with my parents and with my only child and that I could lose them.

126. The night between March 30th and March 31st of 2011 (Moscow time) I called the taxi company from the new phone, which I specifically bought for this purpose, using somebody else's name and address and not stating to the operator as to where we were going. (We knew that these companies were monitored as well and if I used my real name and address, FSB would

find out about it immediately). I met the taxi at the indicated place and then we drove to the place, where Andrey was waiting for us with all our things. This time we had to pack only for carry on, we packed our things considering the fact that it would be dangerous to check in our luggage; we knew that FSB agents watched every airport and they could have access to the luggage of any passenger. Once we left our place, we told the driver that we had to go the Domodedovo airport as opposed to Kiev Station as I have told to the operator. Thus, we were able to get to the airport without any obstacles.

127. We arrived there 2 hours prior to departure (we knew all the departure times in advance), we purchased two tickets from Singapore airlines (since we knew Aeroflot planes had always former KGB agents on board) to Houston and left Russia.

128. However, we couldn't stay at Houston for too long, because the information that we flew out to this city remained in Moscow airport. That is why, despite the fact that we felt really bad, we took another flight to San Diego. The choice of the location was made partially because of the climate, which was recommended by our doctors and partially because our acquaintances lived there; our stay in the United States would be really difficult without their help since we didn't speak English.

129. Nobody knew about our departure: parents, children, friends, in whose apartment we lived beginning February 11th to March 31st of 2011, none of them knew. We didn't have a chance to say goodbye to our relatives. Even now Andrey's and my parents do not know where we are and what's happening to us. And we don't know, for several months now, if they are ok. However, this is a compulsory measure, because it is equally dangerous for them and us to communicate with each other: all phones, electronic mailboxes, and physical mail of our relatives and acquaintances are still monitored by FSB.

130. As a result of Andrey's and my confidentiality and efficiency of our actions, our swiftness, which special services of Russian Federation didn't expect from two seriously ill people, we managed to escape from Russia.

## Life in the United States

131. Andrey and I still shudder if we hear someone speaking Russian. However, I believe that here, in the United States, we have a chance of survival. ...

## Conclusion

132. I started working as a psychologist in private practice in Moscow January 2004 after completing four years of study and kept the practice

until March 2011 when I came to the United States to apply for political asylum. In summary, as a result of FSB actions, my common law husband Andrey is practically handicapped at this time; our parents, our children, our acquaintances, and I suffered from health problems; I lost my property and my possessions; Andrey and I lost our work capacity and the ability to do our research and make money in Russia. I have no reason and no place to come back to. The scariest thing is something else though: I am deeply convinced that if Andrey and I return to Russia after escaping to the United States, it will lead to unavoidable death for both of us and possibly for our relatives and people who are dear to us. Colonel Polunchuk asked Andrey to return to working with the FSB several times after he refused to work with them. He was being given the chance to return to the service of the FSB and chose not to time and time again. His repeated refusals even with all the poisoning showed the FSB he (and I) will never use the Catalog of Human Population  to help the FSB with their criminal activities. Based on this reason, I can't come back to my homeland in any case. I had no interest in coming to the United States until I realized that I would never again be safe in the Russian Federation. I was proud of the work my partner Andrey and I were doing in Russia with the Catalog of Human Population, with our published articles, and with my clients, as well as proud of the hard work realized to enable me to graduate from prestigious and well-respected schools. However, our accomplishments and background have made it unsafe for us to remain in the Russian Federation so Andrey and I both plead for asylum, for safety, and for refuge. I hope to continue my scientific research in the United States and work towards a doctorate's degree.

Thank you for your attention and consideration.

Respectfully,

Olga Vladimirovna Skorbatyuk
Originally drafted July 4, 2011.
Revised and signed February 21, 2012

### Endnotes

[1] His name is Alexandr Gritsak (http://vk.com/id14576155). He is one of the people, whom we suspect were involved in attacks made on our website

and is part of the group led by Colonel A. D. Polonchuk. This group of FSB employees most likely also includes the following people: Alexey Sobolev (http://vk.com/deep_stagnum, http://www.facebook.com/jazz.claimber), Anton Sobolev (http://vk.com/id11648088), Olga Apenko (married name Soboleva - http://vk.com/olga_soboly, http://www.facebook.com/olga.apollin, http://www.facebook.com/olga.apenko), Igor Shushlyapin (http://vk.com/id5387685, http://www.facebook.com/profile.php?id=100005738349182), Rasul Rizvanov (http://vk.com/id16071198, http://www.facebook.com/rasik.dakas), Natalia Hramtsova (http://vk.com/nhramtsova, http://www.facebook.com/natalia.hramtsova), Mikhail Zotin (http://vk.com/id171516, http://www.facebook.com/mihail.zotin.3), Nadezhda Abramova (http://www.facebook.com/nadezhda.abramova)."

# CHAPTER 4

## TESTIMONIAL EVIDENCE FROM POLITICAL CASES OF ANDREY DAVYDOV AND OLGA SKORBATYUK

"I, *<name>*, declare under oath that all information, which is presented in this document, is true.

I would like to tell what happened to my colleagues and what I witnessed.

In 2005, I found out that Russian scientists made a discovery, which became the basis of a unique technology. It allows any person to reestablish the connection with Nature, which is almost lost and which is restricted by our society. Many years of the scientific research and the results of the practical application allowed commencing the compellation of the Catalog of Human Population. http://www.catalogofhumanpopulation.org [Note: the website URL is now http://www.humanpopulationacademy.org] There is no need to mention the significance of such a project for every one of us, who is initially a part of Nature and cannot exist outside its Law. At the time of personal acquaintance with founders of the scientific analytical laboratory "Catalog of Human Population" Davydov, Andrey Nikolaevich and Skorbatyuk, Olga Vladimirovna, I have already used this methodology and had a chance to estimate its high efficiency on my relatives and myself. As a result, I happily met Olga's offer to participate in common projects with the goal of distributing this information. My daughter, *<name>*, joined me in this endeavor. For marketing purposes, we created video materials for Russian speaking audience and created a series of lectures: ...

As a person, who regularly communicated with Davydov A.N. and Skorbatyuk O.V. over a period of several years, I can testify that Andrey and Olga were hard-working and happy people. So it was especially surprising to hear their complaints about the fatigue and indisposition for a prolonged period of time (for example, Olga's malaise began in 2006). It was quiet natural that Olga and Andrey visited doctors, however, treatment modes, which have been offered were not effective.

In August of 2010, after Olga and Andrey came back cheerful and healthy from the tourist visit to the United States, they started feeling bad all of a sudden. This was particularly strange. Every time I saw Olga, I would notice that she had red and irritated eyes and swollen (puffy) face. She was complaining feeling heaviness in her chest, problems with breathing, dizziness, and problems with gastrointestinal tract. At that time Andrey started having suffocation fits. He stopped going outside of the apartment, since he had problems breathing while walking.

My daughter <name> and I tried to help in any way we could. In some time, <name> became ill. She had strange "chills" for a long time and after that she had problems breathing and fatigue for a long time. At the same time, I started having skin itches, I started feeling heaviness in my chest, and after being in the apartment of my colleagues for a long time, I got Quincke's edema. Doctors suggested that it was an allergic reaction. After the fit, I suffered for a long time from eyes colic, reddening of the skin, and heaviness in my chest. It was all really strange, since I have never had allergies before.

We continued seeing medical specialists, trying to find out what we should do in the situation like this. I drove my colleagues, who felt ill, to see the therapist Klochkova, Olga Leonidovna. The therapist suspected that Andrey and Olga were poisoned and gave a referral to see a toxicologist. She warned them, however, that she didn't know for sure, which institution accepted patients with such poisoning. Then my colleagues went to the Sklifosovsky Institute. After hearing their complaints, instead of starting the examination and prescribing certain treatment, the toxicologist suggested the procedure of cleansing of bowels and better yet consult a psychiatrist. After such a blunt humiliation, we decided to start self-examination.

In December of 2010, we conducted a series of examinations. The results were not comforting. At that time, Andrey's bronchial efficiency dropped by 70%. This result was revealed after the spirometry (examination of external respiration function). Other examinations and tests excluded the correlation of such changes and prolonged suffocation fits to asthma, allergy or some serious cardiovascular disease. The examination of my respiratory system revealed obstructive alteration in the bronchial function of the 1st degree (see attachment). However, doctors couldn't explain the reason of such change.

Then we started thinking as to why several people at the same time had problems with health with similar symptoms. Why all of us had problems with phone and internet connection?! We had more questions than answers until Olga, by accident, discovered the break in the door lock to their apartment. It happened on New Year's Eve on December 31st, 2010.

We decided that bad health and housebreaking are linked into the same chain of events and that nobody other than professionals can solve this situation. On January 4th, 2011, Olga Vladimirovna filed an application to the law-enforcement agency. I was present at their apartment when police showed up there. Police officers stated that break-in was very clean and they took the lock with them for expert examination.

After this we immediately contacted the governmental organization, which is dealing with ecology of the residences to conduct corresponding examination. This happened in the middle of January, 2011. The name of this organization is "The Moscow Center for Hygiene and Epidemiology" and it is the leading organization in the city of Moscow. I was present in the apartment during all days, when the examination was conducted. I don't remember the dates, but it happened in January. They probed the air in the apartment and the air near the carpet, which my colleagues took out to the balcony, the air near the bed, where they slept, and the air near the closet in the hallway. Overall they conducted 3 examinations. Beforehand, the experts were using a gas analyzer since nobody knew what kind of substances they were looking for in the apartment.

Having taken required preliminary measurements, the employees of the sanitation and epidemiological laboratory were extremely surprised. The matter is that they have never seen such readings in private residences. The results of object examination shocked not only us but also the experts. They found chemical compounds in the quantity, which is hazardous for life. Maximum allowable concentration of different substances was exceeded by 5, 7, 8, 10, and even 40 times. It was also striking that they found 10 times excess of dibutilphthalate in the carpet, which was rolled up at the balcony in several thick bags. It was bitter frost outside at that time, the windows of the balcony were open, however, it turned out that these substances couldn't be removed by ventilation.

After this examination there was no doubt that problems with health was the result of the exposure to poisoning substances. Andrey started having bronchi spasms more often. I don't want to exaggerate, however, every such fit could become his last. Andrey had cascade blood filtration done. The doctor, who was treating him, couldn't hide her surprise after seeing the color of blood plasma on the plasmapheresis device. After this she insisted on the additional examination. And we were in shock yet again! The unacceptable excess of the quantity of heavy metals in blood was discovered: lead by 40% and cadmium by 20%.

At that time they got rejected in the commencement of prosecution based on the lock damage. This was the end of January, 2011. However, there were enough documents, which supported the attempt of killing people. Olga immediately filed the second application with police with the hope of protection from their end. She made a mistake in her assumption, the police rejected it. There was no examination conducted based on the second application. My colleagues received the second rejection in commencement of prosecution.

Olga was handling the cleaning of the residence on her own. She used dozens of kilograms of detergent and cleaning supplies! Every day she was cleaning almost the entire apartment and rewashed all the cloth. However, it wasn't sufficient. Olga and Andrey had to sleep with their windows open with the temperature following below negative 25 degrees Celsius. (-13 F). In addition, they were forced to sleep on the floor since, first, they threw away the mattress due to its strange smell, and after the examination was conducted, they threw away the bed as well and slept on the floor.

All of a sudden, Olga's daughter Elena Skorbatyuk became ill. She lived separately from her parents in another district of Moscow. She had the same symptoms! The ER doctors rejected the hospitalization, and we urgently moved her in the safe place. We started having scary thoughts. Did they really start the persecution of close relatives?! Olga and I moved Elena to Olga's parents. However, fear of persecution of her daughter soon was confirmed: there were poisoning substances found in the closet where Elena kept her clothing (Olga took it to do laundry).

The letters addressed to superior organizations (MVD, public prosecutor's office) and the letter to the President of Russian Federation didn't change the situation in any way, depriving people of hope of governmental protection. It looked as if authorities and agencies of defense of public order didn't care about the fact that civilians are being killed. There was also an impression that all of those who were contacted by Olga and Andrey didn't want to start the investigation process and, thus, covered up their killers.

All facts pointed out that somebody was trying to deprive my colleagues of their health and, possibly, life. Who is chasing them? For what?! <Name> and I and the multiple acquaintances of Olga and Andrey were trying to answer these questions but all in vain.

One thing I can state for sure that no criminal organization nor simple people would ever be able to do something like that with my colleagues. And this is not my opinion, this is the opinion of experts from the Federal Service on Surveillance for Consumer rights protection and human well-being. Olga and Andrey were asking these experts and I was present at the meeting about who could place the type of substances found in their apartment. The experts' answer was that only professionals could do something like that. Firstly, poisoning substances of this type cannot be purchased at a store. One cannot buy it anywhere. Secondly, experts said, if a non-professional would try to do something like that, without proper training, he would be under the risk of poisoning himself. My colleagues were trying to get the answer from the experts regarding who could be these specialists and where they could be trained, but the experts refused to say anything about it. I don't know about my colleagues, they were always reserved about discussing the events of their past, but I was even more confused by these experts' opinion. It was even harder for me to comprehend what was going on. I was almost certain about one thing: somebody didn't like the research, which Davydov and Skorbatyuk were conducting in regards to the Catalog of Human Population. And this "somebody" wanted to get rid of the research and the research product in the form of the decrypted programs at the same time.

And if this is so, what could happen tomorrow to Olga and Andrey? What could happen to me? To my daughter <name>? To Olga's daughter Elena? To Andrey's children Yaroslav and Vasilisa? To their parents? What if, at some point, this persecution would affect them as well? I was really scared and I didn't know what to do. I couldn't abandon my colleagues in this misfortune, I wanted to help them save their lives, since their research is unique, and they are the only people in the world who are capable of understanding and decoding ancient scriptures. On the other hand, I was incredibly worried about my daughter, my husband, my mother, and myself since if someone would start poisoning me, my entire family would suffer. But one can say I was lucky, nobody was poisoning our house. Most probably only two of our cars were poisoned, mine and <name>'s, since we felt really bad only after driving our cars. And <name> and I didn't directly participate in the compilation of the Catalog, we were only conducting marketing campaign.

As a result, the experts from the Federal Service on Surveillance for Consumer rights protection and human well-being and doctors declared Olga's apartment unusable and hazardous for living there; I invited Andrey and her to live in my apartment. (My family and I mostly lived in the house in the countryside). They didn't want to do it, but there was no other choice. The alternative was simple: either die or leave poisoned premises with all the belongings there. Driven to despair, these people left their apartment at night, leaving all of their belongings behind and moved to my place.

After the move, which took place in the first ten-day period in February 2011, without any protection, Andrey and Olga were afraid to go outside. Living in forced isolation, they were trying to restore their health on their own. Activated carbon, calcium chloride, magnesium sulphate – all of these universal means couldn't substitute the qualified medical help, which they couldn't hope for at this point. The connection to the outside world was established through my daughter and I. We were bringing them groceries and medicine. At that time we weren't even contacting each other by phone and when we saw each other in person, we were communicating passing each other written notes.

Law-abiding citizens of Russian Federation, who have never had any connection to a terrorist organization nor to any criminal structures, were left alone with the terrible problem: constant pressure, fear for their own lives, fear for health and lives of their relatives and close friends! Nobody knew how long all this horror could continue and how it would end for everybody. That is why, one time when I was delivering groceries for them again, I discovered an empty apartment and the note thanking me for everything and apologies for such a sudden departure, and I wasn't surprised with their decision to leave their homeland. Olga and Andrey had nothing else left to do. With such a sequence of events they couldn't expect anything else but death. Perhaps, if somebody were seriously persecuting them, if some professionals were trying to kill them, then sooner or later they would have died.

Everything that you just read is a very brief summary of the events of several months (from August 2010 through the end of March, 2011). I am not going to evaluate these facts. Moreover, I don't know all the details as to why this happened to my colleagues. I would say one thing. I would have never believed that all of this was happening during peaceful times with peaceful citizens in my country if I haven't witnessed it myself and haven't become the participant of these events.

05.21.2011

*<name, signature>*"

# CHAPTER 5

# INTERVIEW WITH ANDREY DAVYDOV

"I began my research in the early 70s of the previous century and it still continues. It started with an astonishing discovery: a Catalog of Human Population does not exist. There are anatomical atlas, catalogs of birds, animals, minerals, plants, machinery, tools, clothing, cars—anyone and anything, but not a human. As far as a human, in addition to the anatomical atlas, there is the theory about races, the theory of four temperaments that came from a doctor named Hippocrates from ancient Greece, and the like. There are also still ongoing debates about the existence of psyche or to put it simply—soul; discussions about what is primary: body or psyche, soul or physiology. There are psychiatry and psychology, which, on the one hand, are considered a science, but, on the other hand, psychologists and psychiatrists themselves state that they are engaged in research of that which they do not have the slightest idea about. Also, there are Sigmund Freud's theories and his student Carl G. Jung's theory, which also state that they are engaged in that which, from their point of view, can only be speculated about. Altogether, a paradoxical situation has formed: a human knows a lot about what surrounds him, about what is in his body, but based in what this body exists, based on what he lives, and why people are different—there is practically no information. And, even more so, there are no plans to scheme out even approaches to the possibility of cataloging humanity by analogy with, for example, the animal world. Therefore, simultaneously, a theory got ingrained that every person is original and unique (and this theory has quite numerous and heavy arguments, namely fingerprints, pinna, blood type). Therefore, many questions why things work as they do led to the beginning of my research: namely, why each person is original, but at the same time is within the common process of natural cycles and has a lot in common with animals, for example. To me, it was a shocking discovery and it prompted me to try to resolve this paradox.

In 1974, after graduating from the People's University Of The Arts Distance Learning Program (panel painting and graphics, Department of Fine Arts), I joined the Union of Artists of USSR. This gave me the ability to access illustrated art albums at central Moscow libraries. First of all, I was interested in artists, who portrayed chimeras of mythological character in their works; where the basic principle was the process of combining different segments of different animals into one creature that did not exist in nature. Nevertheless, their creativity, their works received special attention, were in demand and sellable. This gave me an opportunity to conclude that a viewer shows increased interest in such images. In addition, works of psychologists of the XX century also pointed to an increased interest in the chimerical problematic. Any chimerical diaboliad was and still is especially popular in mass-culture. This phenomenon, as a special phenomenon of viewer's attention, also interests psychologists. Bringing this information into a single whole, it can be concluded that a monster or chimeric approach to the creation of an audiovisual series excites human psychophysiology very strongly. Infatuation of various religious institutions with demonic problematic speaks in favor of this as well.

My avocational research as an artist revealed another interesting fact: mythological monsters are the basis of various kinds of secret, mystical doctrines. They could be considered hobbies of those, who are engaged in this mysticism, but I was surprised by the fact that all developed countries existed and exist on this (mystical) base. For example, the Third Reich, which basically had a mystical platform under its practical developments. This has led to powerful new technological breakthroughs. One of these breakthroughs allowed humanity to go into space, and in particular allowed USA to have such an organization as NASA. Also, this allowed United States to have currency that dominates in the world. It is enough to look at a one dollar bill, where some of the elements are purely mystical. All these scattered facts, which I gathered and analyzed, led me to the question: "Where is the source of mystical, monstrous, demonic, chimerical images?"

In the same year (1974) I came across the ancient Chinese literary record titled Shan Hai Jing (translated from Chinese as the Catalog of Mountains and Seas). All of its content not only consists of mythological monsters, but also is rigorously structured. The idea that this is the source of chimerical images that lie at the basis of the existence of modern civilization came to me then. What remained was to answer the question: "What structure is encoded in this ancient Chinese source?" The underlying idea after the analysis of this ancient book was the thought about nature's existence without humanity and with humanity; although it was totally obvious that the Catalog of Mountains and Seas was made for people and about people and that such fundamental work can be only the Catalog of humanity as species.

At that point I was faced with the following task: to put the question of study of this ancient source onto a professional basis. In my professional development invaluable help was provided by the member of the ITAR-TASS—V. V. Fedoruk, a great scholar of Chinese culture and Chinese language, who shared his knowledge with me; as well as specifics of Chinese modernity, but most importantly—specifics of the ancient Chinese culture.

Research done in our tandem resulted in publications of very first materials on the subject The Ancient Chinese Treatise Called Catalog of Mountains And Seas Is The Catalog Of Human Population in a magazine called Power of Spirit (article was titled Shan Hai Jing: Myths Or Structure Of Psyche?).

Our further research required consultations in regard to other ancient Chinese monuments, such as I Ching and Tao Te Ching. It turned out that there are not many specialists on ancient Chinese culture neither in China itself, nor in Europe, USA, or Russia. However, we were able to attract attention of an outstanding Russian sinologist Anatoly E. Lukyanov. He is a well-known sinologist, scientist-orientalist, professor, the head of the Center of comparative study of civilizations of Northeast Asia at the Institute of Far East of the Russian Academy of Sciences. He was extremely interested in our scientific developments related to the Catalog. Our acquaintance resulted in collaborative work at the International Academy of Anthropology. There was created a research team led by Lukyanov, which included Fedoruk and myself. Together with Anatoly Lukyanov we worked on the topics Shan Hai Jing Is The Catalog Of Human Population and Tao Te Ching Is The Instruction For Shan Hai Jing And I Ching. Work at the Academy as a senior researcher allowed me to become accredited as a participant at the First Russian Philosophical Congress called Human Being—Philosophy—Humanism, which was held in St. Petersburg (Russia) in 1997, and where I gave a presentation about the Catalog of Human Population.

In 2003, one of my clients Andrey V. Varfolomeyev founded a laboratory called Totems (full title: Autonomous Nonprofit Organization—Special Scientific Info-Analytical Laboratory Totems), in which I continued my research. Later on, in 2004, another one of my clients—Olga V. Skorbatyuk, a professional psychologist—joined our laboratory."

# CHAPTER 6

# INTERVIEW WITH OLGA SKORBATYUK

"Many years before I met Andrey Davydov, the discoverer and developer of the Catalog of Human Population, I was seriously concerned with search for working methods in regard to self-knowledge and self-perfection. In search of answers to questions of who I am, what my life's purpose is, and how I can become an individual with new qualities, I examined and tested many methods from psychological, philosophical and religious sources; for example, psychoanalysis, behaviorism, humanistic direction in psychology, Zen Buddhism, Taoism, yoga, Christianity, etc. However, this way led me to great disappointment: in over ten years of searching I did not find anything that would help me get answers to my questions or any specific recipes to solve my problems. Then, I decided to step on the path of a deeper study of the question "what is the soul of a human and what is its structure" and went to a university (Department of Practical Psychology). At that time I was thirty-three years old, my daughter was going through a difficult time called "adolescence," and problems that existed at that time in our relationship also motivated me to gain knowledge in psychology.

However, by the fourth year of my study at the university, I made a final conclusion that knowledge that I have obtained is not able to help me solve even the most basic problems. Not to mention that after these four years at the university, I still did not know who I am, what I was born for, what kind of people surround me, and how to interact with them. I began to look into the future with dismay, as I could not imagine how I would perform my professional duties after graduation and how I would help my future clients solve their problems in life after becoming a professional psychologist. For some time I tried to practice on my friends and acquaintances, and to my horror I realized that the university has failed to provide me with a working method. My concern was shared by many others at the Department of Psychology, especially by those, who like me tried to apply knowledge that they received at the university on practice. For this reason, when in late 2003 I was introduced to Andrey Davydov, the developer of the Catalog of Human Population, and even more so, when I got the confirmation that the methodology works—without delay I began to master it. It helped me greatly that Andrey Davydov accepted my request to allow me to take part in the laboratory's undertakings.

After I began studying the topic of the Catalog of Human Population, I progressed in understanding of what human psyche is and how it functions so powerfully and quickly that while I was still a student at the university, I was able to participate in writing of scientific articles together with Andrey Davydov. We have created a number of monographs:

❖ From Carl Gustav Jung's Archetypes Of The Collective Unconscious To Individual Archetypal Patterns
❖ Archetype Semantics. How It Corresponds To The Concept Of An 'Image': How Archetypal Are Images?
❖ Can Archetypal Images Contain Chimeras?
❖ Society As A Community Of Manipulators And Their Subjects

All of these articles were chapters of a planned book—Textbook Of Non-Traditional Psychoanalysis.

These articles were factually the foundation of a new scientific direction in psychology, created on the basis of decryption of Shan Hai Jing.

After I wrote the first article mentioned above, I introduced it to my supervisor at the university as well as other professors, as Andrey Davydov advised me. I got only very positive feedback in response. My professors were impressed with the depth of subject matter and demonstrated knowledge of the topic. And, according to them, they were also impressed with the fact that a student took part in writing of this level, and that a person with incomplete higher education was able to participate in creation of a product at such level and participate in such studies in general. They admitted that they encountered such a phenomenon for the first time.

My question whether I can use the topic, with which I am engaged at the laboratory (meaning, research of the Catalog of Human Population), caused good-natured laughter by my supervisor, who said: "You intend to write a doctoral dissertation right away? Or maybe you will graduate first?" To my naïve question why a doctorate dissertation specifically, I was told that the volume and level of information that I provided about the Catalog of Human Population corresponds to not even a master's, but at least a doctoral dissertation. In his opinion (which at that time had no traces of influence of the Russian special services observed later), this subject matter was very interesting in regard to developments, as well as its coverage in scientific works. My scientific advisor actually blessed me to make further developments in this field. However, I also noticed that he became especially interested in this technique after I shared with him, with permission of Andrey Davydov, some information from the Catalog of Human Population about him personally, as well as about his wife.

High ratings of my work by representatives of the academic environment (my role at that time was only to describe Andrey Davydov's research product from a purely scientific, psychological point of view) inspired me to continue writing on the topic of our scientific research. At some point I was interested in writing and defending a master's thesis and a doctoral dissertation on the topic of the Catalog of Human Population in a graduate school format. However, the events that have led to my arrival in the United States of America in order to obtain political asylum did not allow me to do this.

After I began working at Andrey Davydov's laboratory, despite the fact that after getting acquainted with the Catalog the knowledge taught at the university ceased to have any information and practical value for me, I completed all six years at this university, passed the exams, and wrote a diploma on psychology of management. After that, as a psychologist, I never returned, neither to study, nor to apply the methods of traditional psychology—I exclusively used the methodology based on decryption of Shan Hai Jing.

After a few years of practical application of the Catalog of Human Population, during work with my clients I never experienced difficulties with use of this tool. I always understood clearly who is in front of me, how to communicate with him or her, had a clear understanding of true motivation of this person, his or her true desires and aspirations, and how I can help. In all of my practice as a psychologist no client has ever left disappointed or dissatisfied. Thanks to my knowledge of research carried out on the basis of decryption of the Catalog of Mountains and Seas—I never felt ashamed of myself and of my work as a professional because it was not based on my subjective view of the client and his situation, but based only on information from the Catalog of Human Population. I think this is why my clients have always been willing to pay quite a high price for information from the Catalog of Human Population about themselves and people who interest them. And, I was always ready to help people, to share with them my knowledge and experience in the application of a unique and universal tool called the Catalog of Human Population, which by a happy coincidence got in my hands.

Neither tragic circumstances, which burst into my life due to interference by the Federal Security Service of the Russian Federation, who tried to kill me, Andrey Davydov, our colleagues and friends (and some, unfortunately, successfully), nor the actual loss of communication with my parents and my only daughter, or the fact that I had to leave my homeland forever—were able to break my researcher's will to continue the study of this ancient source of knowledge about a Human and his "soul," or my desire to participate in the life of the laboratory, which gave me as a psychologist a chance to obtain an answer to the question "what is the soul of a human and what is its structure," and have the widest practical application of this information in my personal life as well as my professional activities. The reason is that I was always aware of the level of the research product that happened to get in my hands, of the value of this product, and what results can be achieved if we continue to research the Book of Mountains and Seas, research of which at the present moment is very far from complete, but clearly shows the depth of knowledge that this amazing book contains.

Although this book has already been marked with the blood of its researchers, and I am not a romantic (I am an analyst), and I realize that by continuing the research of Shan Hai Jing my life will always be in danger—I prefer to spend my life, however long it lasts, on the path of research initiated by Andrey Davydov, but, more importantly, on my personal path to the status of a Human. To me personally this is a more dignified life than life of an animal that knows nothing, does not understand anything, and is a confused, primitive creature, while nearby is the only source in this civilization that was created not by its representatives, and which contains information on how a person can be a Human instead of an animal."

# APPENDIX

# DOCUMENTS CONFIRMING
# AUTHENTICITY OF THIS STORY

## I. Political Cases and Asylum Approvals

### 1. Political Cases

## 2. Andrey Davydov's Asylum Approval

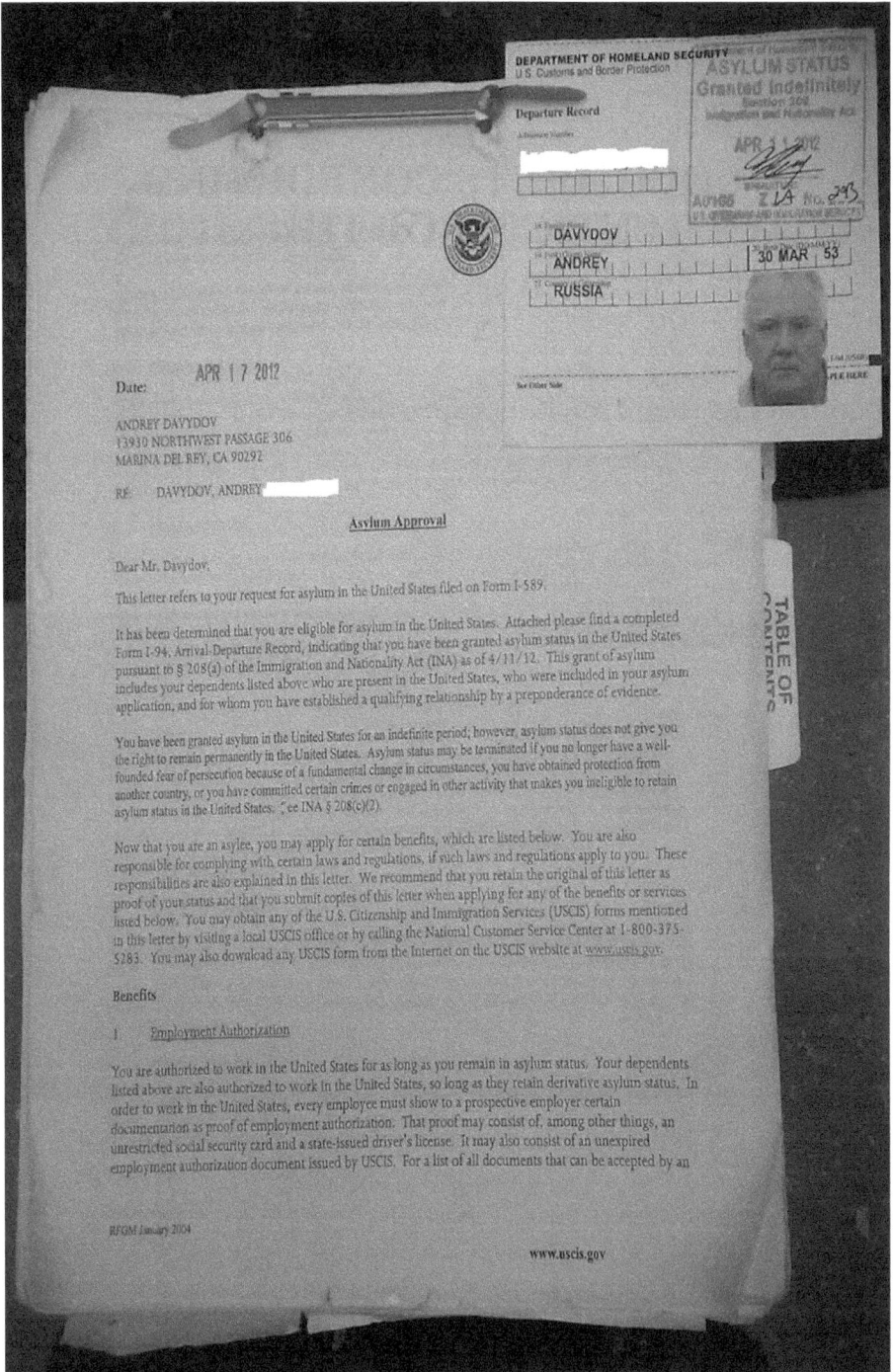

DEPARTMENT OF HOMELAND SECURITY
U.S. Customs and Border Protection

**ASYLUM STATUS**
**Granted Indefinitely**
Section 208
Immigration and Nationality Act

Departure Record

APR 3 1 2012

A0166   Z 1A No. 293

DAVYDOV
ANDREY                     30 MAR 53
RUSSIA

Date:   APR 1 7 2012

ANDREY DAVYDOV
13930 NORTHWEST PASSAGE 306
MARINA DEL REY, CA 90292

RE:   DAVYDOV, ANDREY

### Asylum Approval

Dear Mr. Davydov:

This letter refers to your request for asylum in the United States filed on Form I-589.

It has been determined that you are eligible for asylum in the United States. Attached please find a completed Form I-94, Arrival-Departure Record, indicating that you have been granted asylum status in the United States pursuant to § 208(a) of the Immigration and Nationality Act (INA) as of 4/11/12. This grant of asylum includes your dependents listed above who are present in the United States, who were included in your asylum application, and for whom you have established a qualifying relationship by a preponderance of evidence.

You have been granted asylum in the United States for an indefinite period; however, asylum status does not give you the right to remain permanently in the United States. Asylum status may be terminated if you no longer have a well-founded fear of persecution because of a fundamental change in circumstances, you have obtained protection from another country, or you have committed certain crimes or engaged in other activity that makes you ineligible to retain asylum status in the United States. See INA § 208(c)(2).

Now that you are an asylee, you may apply for certain benefits, which are listed below. You are also responsible for complying with certain laws and regulations, if such laws and regulations apply to you. These responsibilities are also explained in this letter. We recommend that you retain the original of this letter as proof of your status and that you submit copies of this letter when applying for any of the benefits or services listed below. You may obtain any of the U.S. Citizenship and Immigration Services (USCIS) forms mentioned in this letter by visiting a local USCIS office or by calling the National Customer Service Center at 1-800-375-5283. You may also download any USCIS form from the Internet on the USCIS website at www.uscis.gov.

Benefits

1   Employment Authorization

You are authorized to work in the United States for as long as you remain in asylum status. Your dependents listed above are also authorized to work in the United States, so long as they retain derivative asylum status. In order to work in the United States, every employee must show to a prospective employer certain documentation as proof of employment authorization. That proof may consist of, among other things, an unrestricted social security card and a state-issued driver's license. It may also consist of an unexpired employment authorization document issued by USCIS. For a list of all documents that can be accepted by an

RFGM January 2004

www.uscis.gov

## 3. Olga Skorbatyuk's Asylum Approval

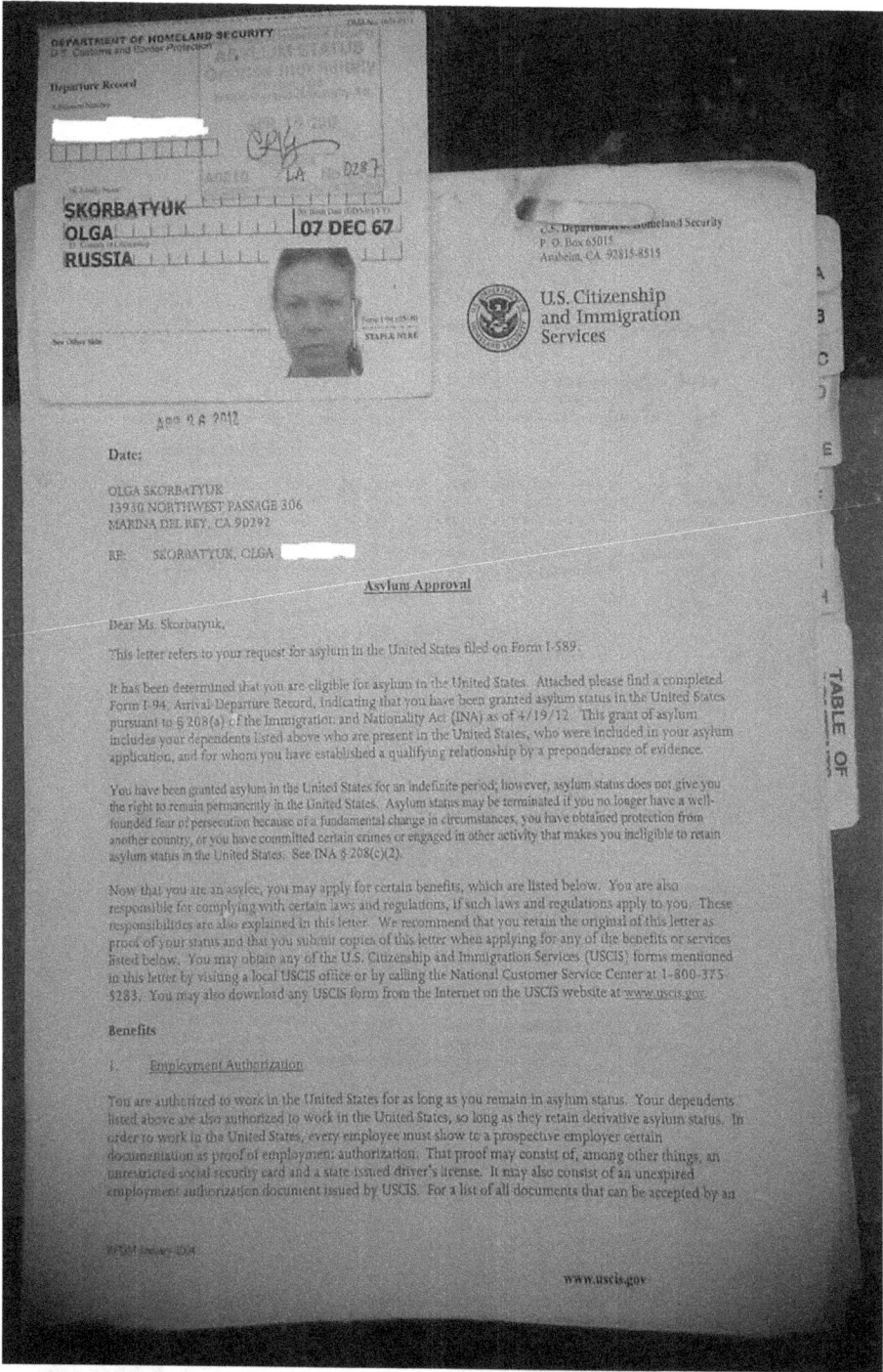

## II. Some of the supporting documents from Political Asylum Applications to U.S. Department of Homeland Security

### 1. Andrey Davydov's Declaration

Andrey Nikolayevich Davydov
13930 Northwest Passage, # 306
Marina Del Rey, CA 90292

#### Declaration

My name is Davydov, Andrey Nikolaevich (Andrey Davydov). I, the undersigned, declare the following to be true and correct to the best of my recollection under penalty of perjury.

#### Introduction

1. I was born on March 30th, 1953 in Frunze, Kirghizia of former USSR (Kyrgyzstan). I was raised in Moscow, Russia, attended good schools, have worked hard in my life, and have no criminal history. I have two children. They live in Moscow. My father is deceased. My mother always lives in Moscow. I currently live at the above address.

2. My partner, Olga Vladimirovna Skorbatyuk ("Olga"), and I came to the United States on B-2 visas on March 31, 2011. She and I are independently asking for political asylum from the government of the United States, in view of the fact that FSB agents (former KGB) are trying to kill us; and it is being done with the furtive consent of Russian government. (Olga's declaration is included with my application and my declaration is included with her application.)

3. Members of the FSB are trying to eliminate me because I provided compromising materials regarding upper Russian executives to FSB Colonel Andrey Dmitrievich Polonchuk. These materials contained opposition research against Putin to show his vulnerabilities and ability to stay in power; the materials were specifically requested by Colonel Polonchuk in furtherance of an apparent plot within the FSB to overthrow Putin shortly after he came into power. It was said in these materials that former President, current Prime Minister of Russia, Putin was a theoretical and practical mastermind behind terrorist acts in his country and abroad. These materials also mentioned the volume of financial means, which Putin possessed: where he took it, how he accumulated it, and how he used it. It was said in the handed over materials that Putin's financial fortune was based on the use of FSB as an instrument to take by force financial means of some Russian citizens, who were illegally transferring large amounts of money abroad from Russian Federation. There was talk of very large amounts. These materials contained the information that citizens who were trying to resist Putin's robbery were eliminated with impunity and their money was transferred to Putin's personal accounts abroad.

4. Additionally, over the span of approximately 5 years I provided other materials to Colonel Polonchuk that I now believe were used for nefarious purposes; including

1

Andrey Nikolayevich Davydov
Declaration in Support of Asylum Application

## 2. Olga Skorbatyuk's Declaration

Olga Vladimirovna Skorbatyuk
13930 Northwest Passage, # 306
Marina Del Rey, CA 90292

### Declaration

I, the undersigned, declare the following to be true and correct to the best of my recollection under penalty of perjury:

#### Introduction

1. I am a forty-four year old citizen and native of the Russia Federation. My complete name is Olga Vladimirovna Skorbatyuk. My birthdate is December 7, 1967. I was born in Moscow. I was raised in Moscow by my parents Vladimir and Yulia. I have no siblings. My parents still live in Moscow. My daughter lives in Moscow. Unfortunately, I have little or no contact with my parents and daughter because I fear that interacting with them will cause them to be targeted by the same group trying to kill me.

2. I came to the United States in 2009 and 2010, both times on a B-2 visa. I did not apply for asylum on either of those trips because at the time I was not completely sure that forces were trying to kill my partner Andrey Nikolaevich Davydov ("Andrey") and I on account of our scientific research, as explained below, and the opposition research he provided to the Russian FSB, as explained below. I then came again to the United States on March 31, 2011 in B-2 status with permission to remain in the United States until September 30, 2011. I came to the United States at that time with my partner, Andrey Nikolaevich Davydov ("Andrey"), so both of us could apply for political asylum together.

3. We have since met with various attorneys regarding our fear of life in the Russian Federation and began to prepare our applications, declarations, and supporting documents, in order to file the documents within one year of our entry to the United States. This declaration is written in support of my application for asylum. As a trained scientist, I have tried to be as detailed as possible, but I can further explain any of the points of this declaration in greater detail if asked to do so.

#### Formal Education and Work Experience

4. I received my formal education in Moscow and attended excellent schools. I received high marks in school and graduated with honors. Growing up, I looked repeatedly for ways to help me with self-realization and self-development. I searched for the answer to the questions of 'who I was,' 'what was my life's purpose,' and 'in what way could

## 3. Indoor Air In Apartment–Lab Test Results

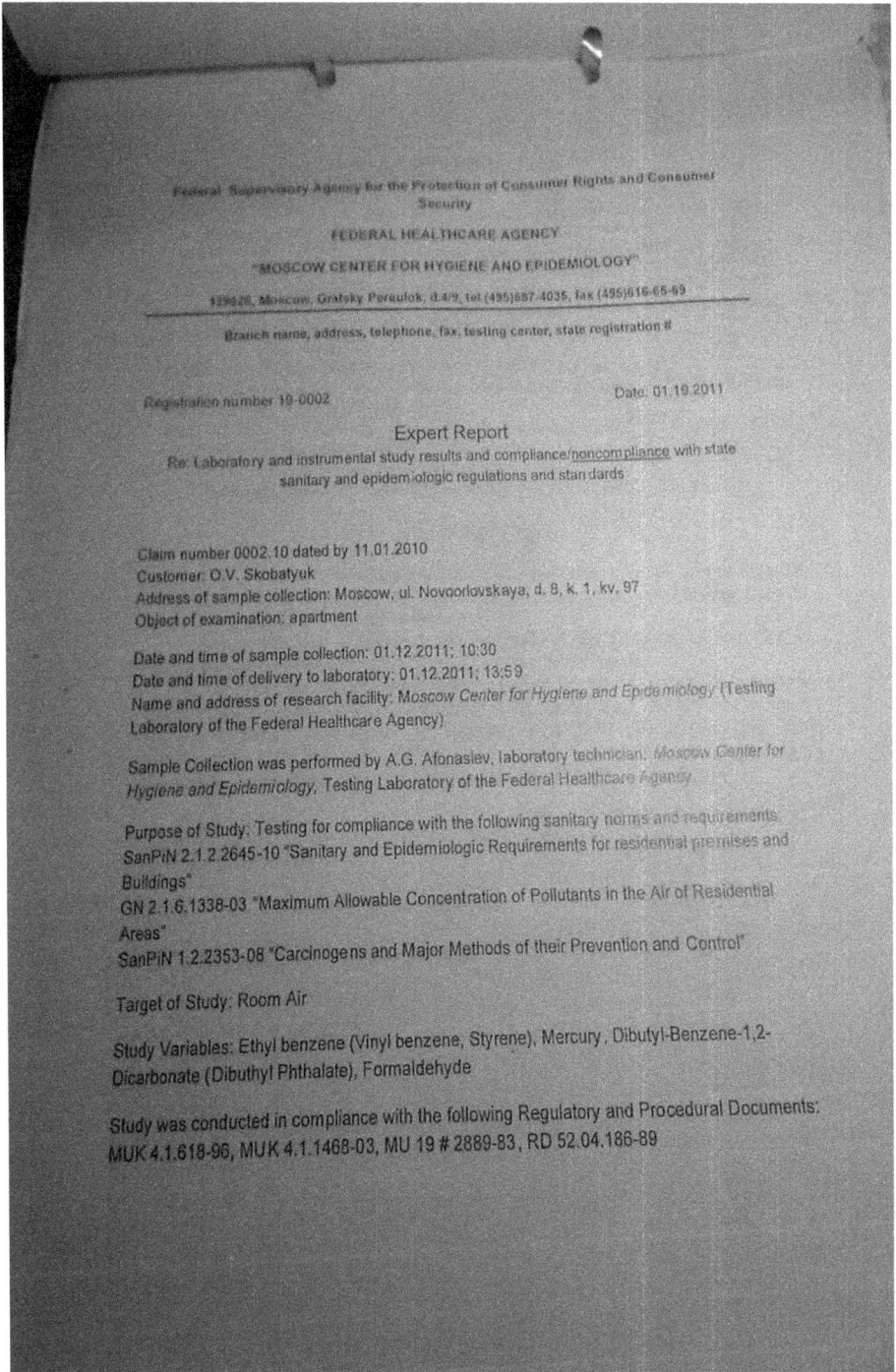

Federal Supervisory Agency for the Protection of Consumer Rights and Consumer Security

FEDERAL HEALTHCARE AGENCY

"MOSCOW CENTER FOR HYGIENE AND EPIDEMIOLOGY"

129626, Moscow, Grafsky Pereulok, d.4/9, tel.(495)687-4035, fax (495)616-65-69

Branch name, address, telephone, fax, testing center, state registration #

Registration number 19-0002

Date: 01.19.2011

### Expert Report

Re: Laboratory and instrumental study results and compliance/noncompliance with state sanitary and epidemiologic regulations and standards

Claim number 0002.10 dated by 11.01.2010
Customer: O.V. Skobatyuk
Address of sample collection: Moscow, ul. Novoorlovskaya, d. 8, k. 1, kv. 97
Object of examination: apartment

Date and time of sample collection: 01.12.2011; 10:30
Date and time of delivery to laboratory: 01.12.2011; 13:59
Name and address of research facility: Moscow Center for Hygiene and Epidemiology (Testing Laboratory of the Federal Healthcare Agency)

Sample Collection was performed by A.G. Afonasiev, laboratory technician, Moscow Center for Hygiene and Epidemiology, Testing Laboratory of the Federal Healthcare Agency

Purpose of Study: Testing for compliance with the following sanitary norms and requirements:
SanPiN 2.1.2.2645-10 "Sanitary and Epidemiologic Requirements for residential premises and Buildings"
GN 2.1.6.1338-03 "Maximum Allowable Concentration of Pollutants in the Air of Residential Areas"
SanPiN 1.2.2353-08 "Carcinogens and Major Methods of their Prevention and Control"

Target of Study: Room Air

Study Variables: Ethyl benzene (Vinyl benzene, Styrene), Mercury, Dibutyl-Benzene-1,2-Dicarbonate (Dibuthyl Phthalate), Formaldehyde

Study was conducted in compliance with the following Regulatory and Procedural Documents:
MUK 4.1.618-96, MUK 4.1.1468-03, MU 19 # 2889-83, RD 52.04.186-89

**Results of Laboratory Tests and Measurements:**
The tests helped establish the following:

1. In the center of the room, the concentration of styrene was 5.5 times higher than MPC; the concentration of formaldehyde was 3 times higher than MPC per the Federal Standard 2.1.6.1338-03 "Maximum Permissible Concentration (MPC) of Polluting Substances in the Air of Residential Areas", Sanitary Regulations and Standards 1.2.2353-08 "Carcinogens and Basic Requirements for the Prevention of Carcinogenic Risks". Concentration of other tested substances in the samples was in conformity with the statutory requirements.

**Regulatory and procedural documents used to evaluate the test results:**
Federal Standard 2.1.6.1338-03 "Maximum Permissible Concentration (MPC) of Polluting Substances in the Air of Residential Areas".
Sanitary Regulations and Standards 1.2.2353-08 "Carcinogens and Basic Requirements for the Prevention of Carcinogenic Risks".

Enclosed: Record of Laboratory Test Results No. ГЦГ23 2011 of 01.17.2011.

## FINDING

The expert evaluation was performed in compliance with the current technical regulations, federal sanitary and epidemiological rules and norms, and statutory standards using duly approved methods and techniques.

The examination of premises was performed at the following address: City of Moscow, Novoorlovskaya ul., d.8, k.1, apt. 97, showed the following:

The indoor air **did not comply** with the Federal Standard 2.1.6.1338-03 "Maximum Permissible Concentration (MPC) of Polluting Substances in the Air of Residential Areas", and with Sanitary Regulations and Standards 1.2.2353-08 "Carcinogens and Basic Requirements for the Prevention of Carcinogenic Risks". Concentration of styrene was 5.5 **times higher than MPC; Concentration of formaldehyde was 3 times higher.**

Chief Physician
(Deputy Chief Physician)                                      A.V. Ivanenko

Specialist of the Communal Hygiene Department                S.A. Rakitin

Chief of the Communal Hygiene Department                     N.V. Kuz

The official round seal "For Expert Reports"
of the Federal Supervisory Agency
for Protection of Consumer Rights and
Security
Federal Healthcare Agency
"Moscow Center for Hygiene and Epidemiology"

# 4. Abstract Of Outpatient Record

MEDICAL SYSTEM
MEDSI
Founded in 1996

### Abstract of an Outpatient Record

02.24.2011

## Patient: Davydov, Andrei Nikolayevich, 57 years old.

Complaints about shortness of breath with labored inhaling and exhaling, painful sensations in chest and neck areas, general weakness, fatigue, dry mouth, recurrent discharge of white "foam" out of the mouth, swelling of the legs (increasing by night time and decreasing by the morning), recurrent convulsive twitches all over the body, numbness of the thumb and index finger on the left hand, intense hair loss within one year, steep body weight increase (20 kg in 5 month); redness and painful sensations in both eyes, tearing.

### Past Medical History:

In the past medical history appendectomy in the age of 16; according to the patient: developmental abnormality – duplication of left kidney. In 2004 – delaminating abdominal aortic aneurysm, endoprosthesis surgery. Last examination of abdominal vessels was performed in 2005. The patient does not take blood-thinning and other medications; smokes; does not keep a cholesterol-lowering diet. No allergies history. No head injuries. Family background: atrial fibrillation (mother).

Weight – 120 kg., Height – 180 cm., Waist line – 134 cm.

### Medical History:

About one year ago – concerns about shortness of breath, weakness, swelling of the limbs. Then the patient spent several months in the USA. Shortly after his return to Moscow (within the last 3 weeks), all mentioned above symptoms came back. The patient indicates feeling unwell after having meals and when exposed to warm temperatures. When experiencing shortness of breath, the patient applies ice in the neck area, and it helps to ease his condition a little. For example he takes, on his own accord, 10% calcium chloratum, 10-15 mg after meals, with milk.

According to the patient, chemical toxicity testing of the air in his apartment, performed by Sanitary and Epidemiological Station, revealed presence of several toxic substances (including volatile organics and formaldehyde), which exceeded their maximum permissible concentration in many times. Partial toxicity elimination was performed on premises.

According to the results of clinic laboratory tests, the patient's hemoglobin level is increased (up to 172 g/l), as well as the numbers of red blood cells and monocytes. Chemistry blood panel showed an increased level of total cholesterol, low density lipoproteins, glycosylated hemoglobin up to 6.8%, hyperenzymemia (increased levels of GGT, ALT and cholinesterase).

Examination of the patient's mineral metabolism showed that lead level in his blood serum was 40%! higher than the maximum permissible, and cadmium level – 20% higher. Zinc level decrease at 35%, selenium – at 35% and potassium – at 6%.

## 5. Diagnostic Lab Test Results

"DIALAB"
Clinical Laboratory Tests

DIAGNOSTIC LABORATORY TEST RESULTS
TO BE USED IN MEDICAL RECOMMENDATIONS FOR TREATMENT OF METABOLIC
DISORDERS

Patient: Andrei Nikolayevich Davydov

Gender: male    Age: 57

Analyzed substance: Blood

M.D. Customer: LLC "MEDSI"

Test No. 00001#15

| 1 | Aluminum | | | | | | |
| 2 | Silicon | | | | | | |
| 3 | Lead | | | | | | |
| 4 | Calcium | | | | | | |
| 5 | Titanium | | | | | | |
| 6 | Chrome | | | | | | |
| 7 | Manganese | | | | | | |
| 8 | Iron | | | | | | |
| 9 | Cobalt | | | | | | |
| 10 | Nickel | | | | | | |
| 11 | Copper | | | | | | |
| 12 | Zinc | | | | | | |
| 13 | Arsenic | | | | | | |
| 14 | Selenium | | | | | | |
| 15 | Molybdenum | | | | | | |
| 16 | Cadmium | | | | | | |
| 17 | Antimony | | | | | | |
| 18 | Mercury | | | | | | |
| 19 | Lead | | | | | | |

MICROELEMENTS

Sample analyzed by: _____    M.D. e Chief Diagnos. S.N. Savenkov

Dept: "DIALAB" CLINICAL DIAGNOSTIC LABORATORY - FOR RESULTS OF LABORATORY Buying

253

# 6. Spirometry Test

Dec 20, 2010

**Ministry of Defense of the Russian Federation**
**Diagnostic and Treatment Center No. 9**
**Department of Functional Diagnostics**

## SPIROMETRY TEST USING A BRONCHODILATION AGENT

| | | | |
|---|---|---|---|
| Last name: | Davydov | ID number: | DA300353 |
| DOB: | 03.30.1953 | Age: | 57 |
| Gender: | Male | Weight: | 120.0 kg |
| | | Height: | 180.0 cm |

DIAGRAM
(Please see original document)

### EVALUATION:

There are moderate (borderline significant) pulmonary ventillatory defects of the mixed pattern, predominantly obstructive. VC is moderately reduced (73%).
Expiratory flow rate in the large bronchi and in bronchial tubes is sharply reduced; expiratory flow rate in the medium-sized bronchi is moderately reduced.

Berotek (200 mcg) was used as a Bronchiodilation agent, with negative (paradoxical) effect.

PHYSICIAN    S.A. SMIRNOVA   /personal stamp and signature/

PHYSICIAN    Leonila Georgievna Yuvakaeva /personal stamp and signature/

BRONCHODIALATOR              12.20.2010        13:23                     1/1

256

## 7. Physician's Referral

AEROLIFE LLC
111020 Moscow
TIN 7722539358
ul. Skotoprogonnaya, d.35, str. 2
tel.: 8-499-739-07-20

### AEROLIFE MEDICAL CENTER

Andrei Nikolayevich Davydov, born in 1953, is hereby referred to F.F.Erisman Federal Research Center of Hygiene.

Ground for the Referral: Possible chronic exogenous intoxications with an unidentified poison.

Purpose of the Referral: Consult with a Toxicologist and with an Occupational Physician to confirm diagnosis and receive treatment.

Date: 12.10.2010          Physician /signature/     O.L.Klochkova

Physician's personal stamp:
"PHYSICIAN* Olga Leonidovna KLOCHKOVA "

# OUR OTHER BOOKS RELATED TO OUR SCIENTIFIC RESEARCH

## Monographic Series

### Archetypal Pattern. Fundamentals of Non-Traditional Psychoanalysis.

Davydov, A., & Skorbatyuk, O. (2014). K. Bazilevsky (Ed.). Anonymous (Trans.). *Archetypal Pattern. Fundamentals of Non-Traditional Psychoanalysis*: *Vol. 1. From Carl Gustav Jung's Archetypes of the Collective Unconscious to Individual Archetypal Patterns.* (Composed 2005. Original work published 2013 in Russian, ISBN 9781301447688.). San Diego, CA: HPA Press. ISBN 9781311820082

Davydov, A., & Skorbatyuk, O. (2014). K. Bazilevsky (Trans.). *Archetypal Pattern. Fundamentals of Non-Traditional Psychoanalysis*: *Vol. 2. Can Archetypal Images Contain Chimeras?* (Composed 2005. Original work published 2013 in Russian, ISBN 978130184859.). San Diego, CA: HPA Press. ISBN 9781310658570

Davydov, A., & Skorbatyuk, O. (2014). Arkhetipicheskiy Pattern. Osnovy Netraditsionnogo Psikhoanaliza [Archetypal Pattern. Fundamentals of Non-Traditional Psychoanalysis]: *Vol. 3. Archetype Semantics: How This Corresponds to the Concept of an 'Image'. How Archetypal Are Images?* (Composed 2005.). Marina Del Rey, CA: Catalog Of Human Souls GP. ISBN 9781301337309

Davydov, A., & Skorbatyuk, O. (2014). K. Bazilevsky (Trans.). *Archetypal Pattern. Fundamentals of Non-Traditional Psychoanalysis*: *Vol. 4. Society As A Community Of Manipulators And Their Subjects.* (Composed 2005. Original work published 2013 in Russian, ISBN 9781301399901.). San Diego, CA: HPA Press. ISBN 9781311809353

## Catalog of Human Population - Non-Fiction Series

### Individual (Subtype) Human Programs

Davydov, A., & Skorbatyuk, O. (2013). *Katalog Chelovecheskikh Dush: Programmnoye Obespecheniye Dushi Muzhchin/Zhenshchin, Rodivshikhsya <Data>* [Catalog of Human Souls: Software of Soul of Men/Women Born On <Date>] (Vols. 1-218. In Russian. Composed 2005-

2013.). Marina Del Rey, CA: Catalog Of Human Souls GP. [Available at http://www.humanpopulationacademy.org/pricing/ in all languages].

## Human Manipulation Modes

Davydov, A., & Skorbatyuk, O. (2013-2014). *Katalog Chelovecheskikh Dush: Kak Podchinit' Muzhchin/Zhenshchin, Rozhdonnykh <Data>. Zhenskiy/Muzhskoy Manipulyativnyy Ctsenariy.* [Catalog of Human Souls: How To Subdue Men/Women Born On <Date>. Female/Male Manipulation Scenario.] (Vols. 1-39. In Russian. Composed 2005-2013.). Marina Del Rey, CA: Catalog Of Human Souls GP. [Available at http://www.humanpopulationacademy.org/pricing/ in all languages].

## Ideologies

Davydov, A. (2014). K. Bazilevsky (Trans.). *Terrorism: A Concept For The ATC (The Commonwealth Of Independent States Anti-Terrorism Center).* (Composed 2001. Original work published 2014 in Russian, ISBN 9781311277848.). San Diego, CA: HPA Press. ISBN 9781310032189

Davydov, A. (2014). K. Bazilevsky (Trans.). *Ideology Of Monarchy. For Office Of The Head Of The Russian Imperial House, Her Imperial Highness Grand Duchess Maria Vladimirovna.* (Composed 2003. Original work published 2014 in Russian, ISBN 9781310150340.). San Diego, CA: HPA Press. ISBN 9781311970152

Davydov, A., & Skorbatyuk, O. (2014). K. Bazilevsky (Trans.). *Ideology Of Religions. Scientific Proof Of Existence Of "God": The Catalog Of Human Population.* (Original work published 2014 in Russian, ISBN 9781311946690.). San Diego, CA: HPA Press. ISBN 9781311413932 ISBN 9780988648593

## Political Science

Davydov, A. (2014). K. Bazilevsky (Trans.). *Essence Of Political Ideologies And Their Role In The Historical Process (Political History Of Russia).* (Composed 2003. Original work published 2014 in Russian, ISBN 9781310199929.). San Diego, CA: HPA Press. ISBN 9781310199929

Davydov, A. (2014). K. Bazilevsky (Trans.). *Influence Of Psychophysiological Specifics Of A Leader On The Style Of Political Decision-Making.* (Composed 2003. Original work published 2014 in Russian, ISBN 9781310037832). San Diego, CA: HPA Press. ISBN 9781310104558

Davydov, A. (2014). K. Bazilevsky (Trans.). *Elitist Political Concepts.* (Composed 2005. Original work published 2014 in Russian, ISBN 9781310223228). San Diego, CA: HPA Press. ISBN 9781310822858

## General Non-Fiction

Bazilevsky, K. (2012). *Human Population Academy: Laws of Human Nature Based on Shan Hai Jing Research Discoveries by A. Davydov & O. Skorbatyuk.* San Diego, CA: HPA Press. ISBN 9781301986781 ISBN 9780988648500

Davydov, A. (2013). *Shan Khay Tszin: Mify Ili Struktura Psikhiki?* [Shan Hai Jing: Myths Or Structure Of Psyche?] (Composed 1999. Originally pub. 1999 in Russian in Moscow: *Power Of Spirit*, 32-35.). Marina Del Rey, CA: Catalog Of Human Souls GP. ISBN 9781301590391

Davydov, A. (2013). *"Shan Khay Tszin" i "I Tszin" – Karta Psikhofiziologicheskoy Struktury Cheloveka?* [Shan Hai Jing and I Ching – Map of Human Psychophysiological Structure?] (Composed 2002.). Marina Del Rey, CA: Catalog Of Human Souls GP. ISBN 9781301510009

Davydov, A., & Skorbatyuk, O. (2014). K. Bazilevsky (Trans.). *AHNENERBE: Your Killer Is Under Your Skin* (Original work published 2014 in Russian, ISBN 9781311356741.). San Diego, CA: HPA Press. ISBN 9781311266682

## A Man And A Woman – Non-Fiction Series

### A Log With Legs Spread Wide

Davydov, A., & Skorbatyuk, O. (2014). K. Bazilevsky (Trans.). *A Log With Legs Spread Wide: Vol. 1. How Men Turn Women Into Nothing.* (Original work published 2014 in Russian, ISBN 9781310388125.). San Diego, CA: HPA Press. ISBN 9781311155771

Davydov, A., & Skorbatyuk, O. (2014). K. Bazilevsky (Trans.). *A Log With Legs Spread Wide: Vol. 2. How Goddesses Are Turned Into Logs. World History Of Turning Women Into Mats.* (Original work published 2014 in Russian, ISBN 9781311238894.). San Diego, CA: HPA Press. ISBN 9781311915603

Davydov, A., & Skorbatyuk, O. (2013). *A Log With Legs Spread Wide: Vol. 3. Women's Thirst For Power Over Men Is The Pathway To Become A*

*Garbage.* (Original work published 2013 in Russian, ISBN 9781301553075.). Marina Del Rey, CA: Catalog Of Human Souls GP. ISBN 9781301435500

Davydov, A., & Skorbatyuk, O. (2013). *A Log With Legs Spread Wide: Vol. 4. The Head – In The Underpants.* (Original work published 2013 in Russian, ISBN 9781301051281.). Marina Del Rey, CA: Catalog Of Human Souls GP.

## Manipulative Games For Women

Davydov, A., & Skorbatyuk, O. (2013). *Manipulyativnyye Igry Dlya Zhenshchin* [Manipulative Games For Women]: *Vol. 1. March 23: Instruction for Exploitation of Men* (2nd ed., in Russian. Original work published 2005, Moscow: SNIALTotems. ISBN 9785716101333). Marina Del Rey, CA: Catalog Of Human Souls GP. ISBN 9781301803521

Davydov, A., & Skorbatyuk, O. (2013). *Manipulyativnyye Igry Dlya Zhenshchin* [Manipulative Games For Women]: *Vol. 2. April 6: Instruction for Exploitation of Men* (2nd ed., in Russian. Original work published 2005, Moscow: SNIALTotems. ISBN 9785716101302). Marina Del Rey, CA: Catalog Of Human Souls GP. ISBN 9781301069286

Davydov, A., & Skorbatyuk, O. (2013). *Manipulyativnyye Igry Dlya Zhenshchin* [Manipulative Games For Women]: *Vol. 3. October 13: Instruction for Exploitation of Men* (2nd ed., in Russian. Original work published 2005, Moscow: SNIALTotems. ISBN 9785716101326). Marina Del Rey, CA: Catalog Of Human Souls GP. ISBN 9781301900824

Davydov, A., & Skorbatyuk, O. (2013). *Manipulyativnyye Igry Dlya Zhenshchin* [Manipulative Games For Women]: *Vol. 4. December 7: Instruction for Exploitation of Men* (2nd ed., in Russian. Original work published 2005, Moscow: SNIALTotems. ISBN 9785716101319). Marina Del Rey, CA: Catalog Of Human Souls GP. ISBN 9781301413065

## Secret Sexual Desires

Bazilevsky, K. (2013). *How To Seduce Men/Women Born On <Date> Or Secret Sexual Desires of 10 Million People: Demo From Shan Hai Jing Research Discoveries by A. Davydov & O. Skorbatyuk.* (Vols. 1-10). San Diego, CA: HPA Press.

Bazilevsky, K. (2013). *How To Seduce Men & Women Born On March 5 Or Secret Sexual Desires of 20 Million People: Demo From Shan Hai Jing Research Discoveries by A. Davydov & O. Skorbatyuk.* San Diego, CA: HPA Press. ISBN 9781301087204

Bazilevsky, K. (2013). *Secret Sexual Desires of 100 Million People—Seduction Recipes For Men & Women: Demos From Shan Hai Jing Research Discoveries by A. Davydov & O. Skorbatyuk.* San Diego, CA: HPA Press. ISBN 9780988648579 ISBN 9781301135035 ISBN 9780988648586

A list of other publications related to our scientific research can be found at http://www.humanpopulationacademy.org/publications/.

# CONNECT WITH US

## 1. Visit our official website.

Human Population Academy and Special Scientific Info-Analytical Laboratory—Catalog of Human Souls: https://www.HumanPopulationAcademy.org

## 2. Connect with us on social networks.

❖ *Facebook* - http://www.facebook.com/HumanPopulationAcademy (Note: you must be logged in to *Facebook* in order to access this page.)
❖ *YouTube* - http://www.youtube.com/user/HumanPopulAcademy
❖ *Google+* - http://plus.google.com/+HumanpopulationacademyOrghumannature
❖ *LinkedIn* - http://www.linkedin.com/company/2484433
❖ *Pinterest* - http://pinterest.com/humanpopacademy/
❖ *Twitter* - http://twitter.com/HumanPopAcademy

## 3. Contact us.

You can find out how to contact us at the Human Population Academy's website under Contacts (see https://www.humanpopulationacademy.org/breakthrough-discovery/contacts/).

# ABOUT US

**Special Scientific Info-Analytical Laboratory—Catalog of Human Souls** was founded by Andrey Davydov. The laboratory is engaged in research and decryption of the ancient Chinese monument Shan Hai Jing, as well as other ancient texts, and creation of the *Catalog of Human Population*. The technology of uncovering individual structures of psyche of *Homo sapiens* for this Catalog was developed by Andrey Davydov; it is not based on any existing domestic or foreign research, methods or theoretical concepts. The laboratory is a partner with the Human Population Academy.

**Human Population Academy** was founded by Kate Bazilevsky. The Academy's mission is to inform all of over 7 billion humans living on Earth about the discovery of the *Catalog of Human Population*. The Academy educates about the *Catalog of Human Population* (*Catalog of Human Souls*) and provides access to informational materials from this Catalog to the public.

## LEADERSHIP

### ANDREY DAVYDOV

**Research Supervisor of the Special Scientific Info-Analytical Laboratory—Catalog of Human Souls**

Andrey Davydov is an expert in Chinese culture, researcher of ancient texts, the author of scientific discovery of the *Catalog of Human Population* and the technology of decryption of the ancient Chinese monument Shan Hai

Jing as the *Catalog of Human Population*. He authored over 300 published books, including scientific monographs and ideologies. In 2012, he was granted political asylum in the USA due to persecution by a group of employees of the Federal Security Service of Russian Federation (FSB, formerly KGB), who decided to expropriate his research product—the *Catalog of Human Population*.

## OLGA SKORBATYUK

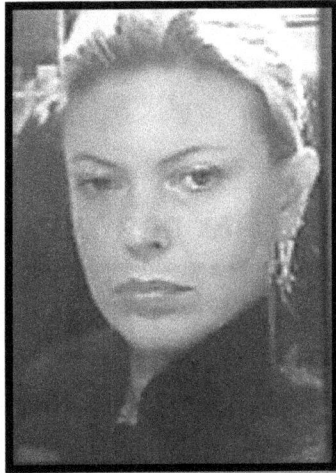

**Senior Analyst at the Special Scientific Info-Analytical Laboratory—Catalog of Human Souls**

Olga Skorbatyuk is a professional psychologist, one of the developers of the *Catalog of Human Population*, the founder of Non-Traditional Psychoanalysis, and co-author of over 300 books and scientific articles. She was granted political asylum in the USA together with A. Davydov.

# KATE BAZILEVSKY

**Founder of the Human Population Academy, Junior Analyst at the Special Scientific Info-Analytical Laboratory—Catalog of Human Souls**

Kate Bazilevsky is the director of the Human Population Academy, a Junior Analyst at the Catalog of Human Souls laboratory, an author and a translator of books about the *Catalog of Human Population*. She holds a degree in MIS and psychology. She founded the Human Population Academy in 2011 and a publishing company called HPA Press in 2012.

www.ingramcontent.com/pod-product-compliance
Lightning Source LLC
Chambersburg PA
CBHW070251290326
41930CB00041B/2441